Rachel's Story

ONE FAMILY'S STORY
OF THE DEATH OF THEIR CHILD

Rita O'Dwyer

VERITAS

First published 2002 *by*
Veritas Publications
7/8 Lower Abbey Street
Dublin 1
Ireland
Email publications@veritas.ie
Website www.veritas.ie

ISBN 1 85390 677 8

Cover design by Pierce Design
Typeset by Louise Baker
Printed in the Republic of Ireland by Betaprint Ltd, Dublin

Veritas books are printed on paper made from the wood pulp of managed forests.
For every tree felled, at least one tree is planted, thereby renewing natural
resources.

*I would like to dedicate this book to
my family here with me,
John, Laura, Bernard and Liam,
and to Rachel, who is waiting for us
in heaven.*

Contents

The Early Years

This is a story about my daughter Rachel, and about a very sad period in my life. Up to the end of 1999, when my life was suddenly turned upside down, everything was fairly normal. When I say normal, I mean as normal as possible for any family rearing four children and coping with a busy workload!

Myself and my husband, John, considered ourselves very lucky at the time. We had four fantastic kids – Laura, Rachel, Bernard and Liam – a good marriage, and a thriving business, which we had started up fifteen years previously in Quilty, Co. Clare.

I used to thank God for all our blessings and never once took anyone or anything for granted. As part of our prayers at night time, myself and the kids had a little one that went like this – 'Thank you God for everything, and please help all the people who aren't as lucky as us!'

The first sad event to touch our lives came in May 1998 when John's mother Kathleen passed away. Even though she was getting on in years, and not in the best of health, her death was sudden and unexpected. Kathleen had lived with us, and she loved her precious grandchildren who meant the world to her. She was a tremendous help to me when they were small and continued rearing and loving them until the end. We had all been so close and when she left us, we couldn't imagine what the house would be like without her. We couldn't figure out how we would get through the following Christmas, the kids' birthdays and just the normal things, like coming home from school and work and her not being there anymore. It was the children's first experience of losing someone close to them and it was a terrible shock. We miss Kathleen so much and still do, but we picked up the pieces and continued with our lives as best we could.

A happy event that comes to my mind is when we celebrated Liam's birthday on 27 August, 1999. Our little family party was also to mark the end of the summer holidays before the older ones returned to school. This was an important year for Laura who was twelve and facing into the grown-up world of secondary school for the first time. Rachel too felt very important at ten and a half, heading into fifth class and into the Master's Room. She would now be the oldest in the family going to national school so that meant she could sit in the front seat of the car on the school run. Bernard was seven and a half and going into second class and looking forward to making his First Holy Communion the following May.

So we had a really lovely day and, like the others, Rachel made sure she got her fair share of sweets and crisps, which she loved. She played with Liam and helped him open his presents and was just as excited as he was.

Rachel just loved these family occasions when we could all be together.

Rachel

Rachel always tended to be on the small side, sort of petite. Maybe she would have grown to be tall, but I don't think so. From an early age she had very long hair, long eyelashes, which everyone used to notice, so she really was a cute little thing! Her hair was a most unusual colour – fair to light brown, but sometimes you could see a red tint and in the summer the sun would bring out blond highlights in it, so different photos show different coloured hair!

When Rachel was three years old we sent her to a local playschool for a year. At this stage she was really quiet and spoke only to people whom she knew well. It was a phase she went through – I don't know if it was shyness or not – she just stared at people, but didn't say a word and wouldn't talk to people.

Around this time Laura used to go to Irish Dancing classes. I used to bring Rachel along and we used to sit on the bench with the other parents and watch the kids dance. It was a lady who taught them, and another girl used to help her. One evening, this girl – Marie – took Rachel out onto the floor and started doing the 'one, two, three' with her and she picked it up straight away. Rachel and herself got on great and it became a weekly routine. I was amazed, first of all that Rachel talked so openly with Marie and secondly that she picked up the dancing so quickly. All the mothers praised her and told me that she would make a great dancer – that she was a 'natural'. I was right proud of her – she was so cute doing her little reel – remember she was only three years old.

Laura and Rachel kept up the dancing for a couple of years and then decided to give it up. I didn't force them. I always tried to give them different options and then let them decide themselves whether or not they wanted to continue. When Rachel was about eight, she suddenly decided that she wanted to go back step dancing so I said OK and made enquiries to see if there were still classes on locally. We found out that the same lady was giving classes at the same place so we headed off one Tuesday evening. We were amazed that Marie was still there and she was delighted and surprised to see Rachel after all that time. She took her aside and started her off at the beginning and by the following week Rachel was doing her little reels and jigs as if she had never stopped. Some of the same parents were still there, and once again they said she was a natural.

Unfortunately after a couple of months, the dancing teacher became ill and the classes had to finish, much to Rachel's disappointment! However, shortly after this Rachel and her friend Niamh decided to go to another dancing teacher and again, she took to it straight away and loved it and the two of them headed off every Tuesday evening.

Niamh and Rachel were very good friends and had a lot in common. They were in the same class at school and visited each other in the evenings and at weekends. They often had 'sleep overs' at each other's houses and had great plans and dreams for their future. They both served Mass on Saturday evenings and if Rachel caught me not looking at her, I would hear about it after Mass. She loved to be the centre of attention. She loved people to notice her and she loved to feel important. Niamh's older sisters, Davina and Ashling, were our regular babysitters and Rachel and the others were cracked about them. Rachel couldn't wait until we were gone out for the night so that she could get on with the job of getting her little nails painted and her hair done. Because Rachel had such long hair, Davina used to do it up in different styles every night. When I would get back, she would always look beautiful and so grown up.

Other times, Niamh would be over and they would dress up and put on make-up and it was so funny to hear their conversations.

Rachel and Laura shared a bedroom and even though they fought like cat and dog at times, they were very close. Rachel looked up to Laura so much and admired her and I would say her main aim in life was to be like Laura. She loved to be included in the things Laura was doing, and couldn't wait until she was in secondary school like Laura. Often late at night I would hear them chatting away and as soon as they would hear me coming, I would hear the click of the light switch and they would pretend to be sleeping. They used to go on holidays together in the summer to their grandparents in Mayo for a week and they used to have such fun.

Bernard and Rachel were close too, but one wouldn't see that all the time! When there were others around, Rachel wouldn't think it very cool to be on friendly terms with her younger brother. There would be terrible slagging between them and often Rachel would come to me and say, 'Please get rid of Bernard – he's annoying me!' However, when it was just the two of them they would play away and make up some great games – Rachel had a great sense of adventure and had a fantastic imagination. She used to make up stories. She wrote several short stories that were really funny and lots of little notes to me, which I used to find in the most unusual places. As she got older, she would write these stories and letters on the computer using fancy lettering and colours. I used to tell her that when she grew up she would be a famous writer and people would be crowding around her to get her autograph.

I think it was Liam that had the special bond with Rachel – they were very close. She was like a little mother with him and kept him occupied for hours at a time. He was stone mad about her and sometimes he would have kisses for Rachel and he would have none for the rest of us. Lots of times in the evenings when I would be trying to do homework with Bernard at the kitchen table, Liam would be trying to climb all over me looking for attention, Rachel would say 'It's OK, Mam. I'll look after Liam', and she would have him up on her hip and I could get on with the homework. She used to look so comical as she was small and Liam was a big child, yet it was no bother to her to keep him up in her arms for ages.

Even Malty, our little dog, had a great thing going with Rachel. We got the dog as a family pet, but it was Rachel that sort of took charge and it was Rachel who used to tear around the place with Malty running around after her. They had such fun and she was really cracked about him. He used to sleep in her room and couldn't wait until she got up so he could have fun with her.

I could go on and on about the different people who knew Rachel and who were touched in a special way by her. She was a very special little girl and anyone who knew her was cracked about her. She was very funny and loved telling and listening to jokes. She would do anything for a laugh and loved playing tricks. Often at work I would hear the front door open and look up but no one would be there. Five or ten minutes later, she would jump out at me and frighten the life out of me. She would then go on to say 'Hi Mam! I'm bored, can I stay here and help you in the office?' I would let her sit at the desk and she would write letters to me – small, funny notes with really bad spellings, but ones that I still have and will treasure forever.

Sometimes she might be a bit upset about the kids at school slagging her about a particular 'boyfriend'! She used to tell them that she had her own special boyfriend – the son of a friend of mine whom she met briefly when they were both babies. She was delighted to have this name to brag about and of course none of them knew this 'super cool guy'. Many a time, I told Rachel that when she was older her Prince would come on a white horse and whisk her off to his castle in the clouds. I don't know where I got this from but I said it her so many times, even when she was older and it always put a smile on her face and it was a special little thing between us.

Rachel absolutely loved when we were all together as a family. Because we both work full time, this would be mainly at weekends and she would be delighted when we would head off on a Sunday morning for a day out, or weekends when we would go away. She used to have endless fun swimming with John and the others and the rougher John was with her, the more she loved it. He used to pick her up in the pool and throw her and her screams and laughter could be heard all over!

She became involved in swimming and joined the club Laura was with. She was very good at it and, no more than the dancing, she would have gone on to become an excellent swimmer. Rachel's other main hobby was reading – she always had a book on the go, especially at night and many a night I would go in to say goodnight and she would have fallen asleep with her book in her hand and the light on.

At school she was what you would call average – not the best in the class, but not the worst either. Every day when she would sit into the car after school, she would be bursting with news, telling me all that happened during the day, giving out about the teachers usually, or telling me about whoever got into trouble. Of course I didn't always have the honour of being on speaking terms with her – when we would have a row or if she was mad at me then I was in the 'dog house' and I would get the silent treatment. This could go on for a couple of days sometimes and in the mornings when she would get out of the car, I would get no kiss and no response when I would ask her if I could get out of the 'dog house' soon. However I used to watch her going in the gates and she would be doing her very best to keep a serious face on and I would always catch her giving me a quick glance and she would be ready to burst out laughing. She could never stay mad at me for long and I was the same, as you would have to laugh at her – she was so full of fun and mischief and up to every trick.

I always say that our kids bring out the best and the worst in us. If I was to try and remember the time I got most angry with Rachel,

I'd say it was when she was about five years old and Laura was six and half. Laura cut Rachel's fringe and what a mess she made – it was completely crooked and botched! The two of them came down to me at work and thought I wouldn't notice. I nearly hit the roof – I was so mad at Laura for doing it and mad at Rachel for letting her do it. I roared and shouted and sent them to their room – they didn't realise I could get so mad. Of course we laughed about it later but at the time it definitely was not funny and it took ages for her hair to grow back. At this time Rachel was also missing her two front teeth and had a cut on her nose so the poor thing looked very comical!

I have no problem remembering the funniest thing that ever happened regarding Rachel. We had (and still have) a little tradition in our house whereby when one of the kids would lose a tooth, the tooth fairy would come and leave a letter and some money. They each had their own fairy and before their tenth birthday, they would get a letter stating that there would be no more letters, but they would still come and leave the money. Rachel's fairy's name was Nancy and Rachel used to write back to Nancy and leave the note under her pillow. One night when Rachel was ten she put her tooth under her pillow and decided to stay awake all night to see this Nancy, or whoever came to take away the tooth. I called into the room around twelve o'clock and there she was, sitting straight up with her book and she hadn't a notion of going to sleep. I said good night and went to bed myself, setting my alarm for two o'clock. I sneaked in and as sure as anything she was still awake so I set my alarm once again for four o'clock and at long last her eyes were closed. I sneaked in and put my hand under the pillow to take away the tooth and left the pound. All of a sudden she shot up in the bed and shouted 'Gotchya!' Well, I never got such a fright in all my life and all I could do was laugh. She kept saying 'I knew it was you! See, I caught you!' I did my very best to stay serious and tried to convince her that I was in checking Liam and I just called in to pull up the quilt on her, but she wouldn't believe me.

The following morning I was taking herself and Laura and their cousin to the train in Ennis, as they were going to Dublin for a few days. Rachel still wanted me to tell her what I was doing in her room the previous night and I still stuck to my story. This went on all the way to Ennis. Just as we were getting near the train station, she asked me one more time – 'Mam, tell me there are no fairies – tell me *now*!' Of course once again I said that there were fairies, and next thing, she stuck out her hand and opened her fist and there was the tooth and she said, 'You're wrong! See this, it *was* you last night who left the money!' You see, when I took the piece of tissue, I never checked to see if the tooth was actually wrapped up in it and never realised that Rachel (clever girl that she was) had taken the tooth and kept it in her little fist all night and all morning and left it until the very last minute to produce it and prove me wrong. I laughed so much and had to admit that she got me good!

I could go on and on about the different times when she made me laugh and when she made me cry, but I won't as a lot of these little stories might only have special meanings for me. I think it is now time to start on the main purpose of this story. I am not sure if I will be able to write the words that are in my head and in my heart, but I will try my best. I kept a brief diary of the daily happenings over those couple of weeks and I will refer to that for specific details if I need to.

The First Symptoms

On Saturday 23 October 1999, Rachel had a swimming gala in Shannon. Laura goes to these galas on a regular basis, but Rachel hadn't been to too many. I volunteered to go as I felt Rachel was a bit young to go without me, and anyway, a certain amount of parents have to go. So we headed off early Saturday morning from Lahinch and Rachel was in great form – better than me as I always find galas very long, you are inside by a pool all day, and the noise level is always so high. Rachel was friendly with another little girl from the same club and they did their races and enjoyed themselves. She didn't win any medals, but she swam well and I was proud of her and glad to be there when she reached the end. She always gave a look up to make sure I was looking at her and cheering for her! I chatted away to the other mothers and before long we were heading home again, stopping as usual at Supermacs for chips.

By the time we got home we were both exhausted. Rachel said she had a pain in her head and that she would lie down on the couch for a while. That's what I felt like doing too, but I had to get the house organised and get something to eat for the others. Later on when I had the boys in bed, Rachel woke and said she didn't feel well. I still reckoned that it was tiredness after the day, so I took her up to bed and told her she would feel fine in the morning. A couple of hours later she woke up and said she felt awful. I took her temperature and it was a little high. I gave her a Panadol and she slept well for the rest of the night.

The following morning we all had a bit of a sleep in and when Rachel woke she seemed to be in fine form with no pain. However as soon as she got up to go the toilet she felt dizzy and vomited a little. So I rang to see if there was a doctor on duty. There was, so I took Rachel in to Milltown and a young, lady doctor examined her. She thought Rachel might have a kidney infection and asked for a urine sample. Poor Rachel couldn't do this so the doctor said she would call out to the house later on and in the meantime gave us something to stop Rachel getting sick.

So we got home and I made a fuss of Rachel and made her a little bed on the couch and she watched television. Later on I got the urine sample from her and had it for the doctor when she called later on. The doctor confirmed that it was a kidney infection and gave me antibiotics, so I was glad it was looked after. That week was the November mid-term break so there was no' school, which also meant no pressure in the mornings getting them up early and no rushing in the evenings trying to get homework done and getting them to bed in time. I always say that these breaks mean more to us parents than they do to the kids!

On Monday she was better, almost her usual self. She slept in late like the others and did normal stuff during the day like playing the Playstation and watching television. On Tuesday she was fine and told me she would be going to her usual set dancing classes that evening. I suggested she skip her class, but she said 'No way' – that she would miss a step and might fall behind. When I called in to watch the dancers, I noticed Rachel was a little pale and at the break she came over and sat on my knee. I admit I was a little worried and was sorry I didn't make her stay at home, but after a few minutes she bounced up again and danced away until the end of class. On Wednesday she was fine – no complaints and she played away with the others.

By Thursday 28 October Rachel was on the last of her antibiotics and said she would go swimming. Again, I tried to persuade her not to go, but she insisted and I eventually agreed. I warned her to get out of the pool if she felt tired or if she wasn't up to it. She and Laura came back around 8 o'clock and Laura's friend Selina was with them as she was having a sleep-over. Rachel said she had a pain in her head so I told her go in and lie down on the couch in front of the fire and have a rest.

Late that night I called in to the girls' bedroom. Laura and Selina were in the double bed chatting away and Rachel was in the single bed. I said goodnight and asked them if Rachel was sleeping. She stuck her head up and said she wasn't, but I could tell she was nearly there and said good night to all three and told Laura not to have the light on for too long.

I went to bed myself then and was asleep before long. I woke up later to find Rachel standing beside the bed saying she was thirsty. I looked at the clock to see it was two o'clock and told Rachel there was a bottle of 7-Up on Daddy's side of the bed, so she went over and took a drink. I asked her if she was OK and she said she was, said good-night to us and headed back to bed. I thought the whole incident was a bit strange, as when the kids were smaller they were always in the habit of coming in during the night if they had a bad dream or if they needed something – in fact Liam still often comes in for a cuddle – but the girls were past this stage so it was very unusual for either of them to come in to us during the night. I had just started to drift back to sleep when Laura came rushing into the room saying Rachel was choking or something. I ran to their room with John behind me – Rachel was lying in her bed with her eyes open, but she seemed to be in some sort of trance. She was making jerky movements and there was some froth around her mouth. My first thoughts were that she was having a bad dream and I tried to wake her, saying, 'Rachel! Wake up, wake up! Mammy's here.' Realising that this wasn't the case, I took her up in my arms and took her to my bed. I don't know why I did this – I just thought our bed was safer and that she would be OK there.

After a few minutes I realised that there was something seriously wrong. I had never seen anyone having a convulsion or a seizure, but I figured this is what was happening to Rachel so I rang the doctor and told him what was happening. Our regular doctor was off duty. I got through to another doctor who told me that it was common enough for kids to get convulsions and that he would come out, but we would still have to go into hospital so she could be checked out. John held Rachel while I got dressed and I held her while he got dressed. I rang my friend Irene who came over to stay with the others. Poor Laura and Selina were really frightened and didn't know what was going on. The doctor came and gave an injection to Rachel. She screamed out and I was glad to hear this as I knew her senses were coming back – before she hadn't responded to us in any way. We headed off to Limerick hospital, John driving, me in the passenger seat with Rachel in my arms with her dressing gown wrapped around her. She had fallen into a sleep at that stage and it was a very dark, silent journey at three o'clock in the morning. Both of us were filled with our own thoughts, praying that there was nothing serious wrong with our little girl, but not convinced. We had never been through anything major with our kids and never spent a night in hospital with them. We were blessed up to then.

Rachel's Stay In Limerick

As we drove through Newmarket-on-Fergus, Rachel woke up and started to cry and managed to tell me she had a pain in her head. I tried to comfort her as best I could and kept telling her that we would be at the hospital soon, that the doctors would make her better, that everything would be all right and that we would be back home soon. She cried and cried until we got to the hospital. I was nearly crying myself from not being able to comfort her. John pulled up right at the main entrance to the hospital and I carried Rachel in while John parked. She was still crying and I found it hard to carry her, but at that hour of the morning, it was quiet and someone came and took her from me straight away. She was taken into a room and some nurses started asking questions that seemed to go on forever – the same thing over and over again. Different people kept coming and examining her and told me they couldn't give her anything for pain until they knew what was wrong.

Their first worry was meningitis and they kept repeating those tests and looking for signs for a rash, which didn't appear. Rachel was still crying with pain. Eventually, after a lot of form-filling and questions being answered, she was admitted. John went home around seven and they got Rachel settled in a ward and I sat beside her. At this stage they had given her something for pain and she was sleeping. They put her on a drip – just a saline solution – and I was told the doctor would be around later in the morning and by then the results of the various blood tests would be back.

I started to breathe easy for the first time and thought to myself, 'Thank God! Panic over.' Whatever had happened was over and Rachel was sleeping peacefully. I started to look around then – it was still early morning and there were a couple of other kids in the ward. As the morning moved on, the nurses changed shift, kids woke up and the place became alive. Rachel still slept, but I didn't worry too much over this as I reckoned she had a good bit of sleep to catch up on. Later on she did wake and I walked her down to the bathroom – her drip was on a mobile unit. When I had her settled back to bed I told her what had happened and she told me what she remembered, which was very little. She said she felt OK and apart from being a bit sleepy I thought she looked alright and wasn't concerned – I was so glad that she was talking to me and apparently over whatever had happened.

Rachel said she wasn't hungry and just wanted to sleep so I told her sleep away and that I would be there whenever she woke. Before she went asleep she asked for her Daddy and wanted to know when he was coming in to see her and whether Laura, Bernard and Liam would be in. Rachel loved attention and even in her hospital bed she felt very important with her drip and wanted everyone to see her and give her loads of attention. I assured her that John and Laura would be in for sure, but that it would be too late for the boys. This satisfied her and she made herself comfortable with her hand under her jaw and fell asleep.

I took a walk down to the shop, made some phone calls, and got some magazines for myself and Rachel, and some sweets and Jaffa Cakes and went back up to sit with her. Around 11 o'clock the doctor came and spoke to me. He said that it wasn't unusual for kids Rachel's age to get convulsions and that it might be just the one, or else it could be the start of epilepsy, which can start at that age. He said the fact that she hadn't had any further convulsions was a good sign and that they would keep her in that night and monitor her and if all was well the following day we could go home.

Naturally I was thrilled with this news, although I was a bit frightened at the thought of Rachel being epileptic. However I tried to dwell on the theory that it was a once-off case and looked forward to going home on Saturday, the following day. Of course then I started thinking about work, and how I would be two days behind and that the accounts would be late going out. Silly things to be thinking about, but at the time I didn't think they were silly.

Rachel slept through dinner – I didn't wake her as I reckoned the sleep would do her good and, after all, she had had very little the previous night. During the afternoon she woke and sat up in the bed and seemed to be OK, again asking when the others were coming in. I asked one of the girls to bring her a cup of tea and toast, but she only took a sip from the tea and bite from the toast. We went down to the bathroom again and we chatted away. When we got back to the bed I showed her the magazines I had got and she looked through them. I knew she wasn't back to normal, but we had a bit of a laugh together and I wasn't too concerned. That evening John and Laura came in and Rachel was delighted to see them. They brought her in some cards from home, and she was delighted with herself and the fact that she was the centre of attention. She showed Laura her drip and how she was able to walk down to the bathroom with it. They ate sweets and we all chatted and had fun and before we knew it, it was time for them to go. John had brought me in a fold-up bed, which I set up beside Rachel's bed and after they went home I said good night to Rachel and settled down on my mattress. I wondered if I would get any sleep with the little fellow next door in his cot making an awful racket.

My mind was filled with so many different thoughts, but my main one was the fact that we would be going home the following day and I was thankful to God for that. I am not sure what was on Rachel's mind before she fell asleep, but I know she was really looking forward to going 'trick or treating' for Halloween the following Saturday night with Niamh and also going away to Killarney the following weekend.

At some stage I drifted off to sleep and the next thing I knew I was awake and could see three nurses around Rachel. I knew something was wrong. It was around 2 o'clock. I jumped up and asked what was wrong and one of the nurses said that Rachel had wet the bed and they were trying to change the sheets. I tried to wake Rachel up and make her realise what had happened. It never dawned on me that the reason she had wet the bed was that she had had another seizure and bed wetting is one of the after-effects. I just thought that she would be so embarrassed when she realised what had happened. I got her up and managed to walk her down to the toilet and kept saying, 'Come on, Rachel. Make your wee-wee and then we'll go back to bed.' She didn't make anything and didn't say a word and seemed to be dazed, but again I was so convinced that all was all right. I just reckoned that she hadn't woken up properly and took her back to bed. I tucked her in and said good night and got back down on my own bed. It's always so scary when something happens at night time and I was a bit anxious, but still looked forward to the following day when we could go home and put this all behind us.

A couple of minutes later I heard Rachel moving and sensed immediately that, yet again, there was something wrong. I got up and went to Rachel who was lying with her back to me. She was having a seizure – her face was in a trance and her arms were jerking. I called for help and two nurses came straight away. They took Rachel down to a little room and by then the seizure had stopped. By this time I had begun to recognise the signs and symptoms before, during and after a seizure. I could see that the nurses were getting a little worried and decided to call in the doctor on duty. He said they would monitor Rachel closely and if she got any further seizures he would start her on medication to prevent any further attacks. After the seizures Rachel would go into a deep sleep. While she was having them, her eyes would be open and her mouth would froth a little and sometimes her arms and legs would make jerky movements. I found it very frightening to watch these and just wanted them to stop.

After about twenty minutes the nurses decided to bring her back down to the ward and we had her just settled in bed when she suffered her third seizure that night. This one was much the same. The nurses kept asking me what did I notice moving – her left or right arm, her left or right leg, what parts of her face, so I knew what to watch out for during the seizures that followed. We took her down to the little room again and this time the doctor started her on treatment to stop the seizures. It had no effect, as she had three more during the night. By the time seven o'clock came I just didn't know what on earth was going on. I rang John and told him what had happened. He was so shocked, as everything seemed to be OK when he was in the previous night. He said he would come straight in and that we would talk to the doctor and find out what the story was. At this stage I knew that my plan for going home was not going to happen and my fears and worries started to make me feel very scared and anxious. At this stage Rachel was sleeping – I wasn't sure whether this was a normal sleep or if it was the after-affects of a seizure. She was still getting them. When John came in, the paediatrician on duty for weekend talked to us. Dr Mahony seemed to be taking things very seriously, first of all he told us that Rachel would be getting her own room with a full-time nurse. He explained to us that at this stage they didn't know what was causing the seizures and they were concerned about not being able to control them. He told us that Rachel would be going for a CAT scan, possibly a lumbar puncture and various other blood tests. We were fairly confident that by the end of the day we would have some definite results.

We felt that things were in control and that Rachel was in good hands. Of course that didn't stop us from worrying, but at least we felt something was happening. We sat at each side of the bed in her own room, while the CAT scan was being organised. Because it was Saturday people had to be called in especially for the job and the person who reads the scans had to be called in also. The bed-wetting continued with each seizure and after a lot of changing of sheets and underwear, it was decided to use nappies. Myself and John were concerned about what Rachel would think when she woke up, but the nurses assured us that they were only while she was in her deep sleep and once she was on the road to recovery she wouldn't need them and she wouldn't find out that she had been wearing them. At one stage I was going out to make a call and I noticed that there was a sign on her door – ISOLATION. I figured that this was on the door for whoever the previous patient was in that room, but later realised that this was for Rachel and that she was allowed no visitors apart from myself and John. This really frightened me.

I made some phone calls during the day, to Laura and the boys, to the girls at work and to my own mother who was shocked to hear what was going on. She offered to come down but there was no point really, as we didn't know what was happening and I told everyone to hold on until we had something definite to tell them. We kept talking to Rachel and in between her seizures and her sleep, she could hear us and knew we were there. We kept trying to reassure her, and told her what was happening as best we could. She had a drip and a little monitor attached to her finger and Rachel always had a habit of sleeping with her fist curled up under her jaw and she kept doing this and knocking off her little monitor. After a while we were told the CAT scan was set up so off we went. I never saw a piece of equipment like it, but everyone explained the procedure to us. It was important that Rachel kept very still while she was in the 'tunnel'. John and I were on either side of her, but as she was still getting the seizures it was very difficult to keep her still. Eventually they got the job done and we took her back to the room and waited for the results.

Nothing major showed up. Apparently they thought they might find a tumour, or an abscess on the brain or something abnormal and they didn't. We weren't aware of these possibilities until the different nurses involved came over and said, 'Thank God nothing showed up!' There was a great sense of relief, but we still had nothing to go on and had no reasons why Rachel was getting so many seizures. The rest of the evening was spent much the same way – the dreaded seizures still coming, the sleep afterwards and then waiting for the signs of the next one, which always came. We decided that I would go home and get a night's sleep and John would stay. I hated leaving her, but knew that one of us should be at home with the others to let them know what was happening. It is always so hard for the people at home and it is not always easy to talk on the phone. Earlier in the evening one of the nurses whom we know mentioned the word 'encephalitis' to us. I had never heard of this and hadn't a clue what it was. At the time we didn't take much notice and didn't investigate it further – it was only later on that I remembered her words.

I drove home and the kids were so happy to see me and, of course, full of questions about Rachel. I told them what I knew. We have always been honest with our kids and I explained things as best I could, but there were so many unanswered questions, like 'When is Rachel coming home?', 'What's wrong with Rachel?', 'Why is Rachel in hospital?', 'Why do you have to go back tomorrow?', and on and on. I spent some time with Liam and told him his stories and eventually got him to sleep. I then spent time with Laura and Bernard and tried to reassure them and promised them they could come and see Rachel as soon as she was out in the normal ward again. A lot of phone calls came and it was so frustrating not being able to explain what was wrong with my poor little girl. Later on my friend Rita called. She had been away and had only just heard what was going on. We had a cup of tea and I told her everything that had happened. I rang John several times and things were much the same – she was still having the seizures and the medication didn't seem to be controlling them. I got a little sleep – it was lovely to be in my own comfortable bed, but so awful to be away from Rachel and John. I tossed and turned a lot, and so many things were going though my head. I was trying to stay calm and kept saying to myself that this wasn't serious – she would be OK. I tried to pray, but couldn't concentrate.

The next morning John rang with some news – they had come to the conclusion that Rachel had this encephalitis and, to control the seizures, they had decided to put her on a drug called Medazalin, which is fairly strong and can affect the breathing. So as a precaution she would have to be put on a ventilator, and to be put on a ventilator she would have to be moved to intensive care. Now the words 'ventilator' and 'intensive care' should have frightened me I suppose, but the way it was explained to John and the way he explained it to me, it all made sense and I never for a moment associated the ventilator with a life-support machine. I was thankful that all this was happening and felt very hopeful that she would improve immediately on this strong drug. I told all this to the kids and said goodbye to them, explaining that Daddy would be home that evening. We knew that this was going to go on for a few days, so we decided that we would take it in turn so that one of us would be with Rachel and the other at home with Laura, Bernard and Liam.

When I arrived back at Limerick Hospital, John and I spoke to Dr Mahony again and he explained to us what encephalitis was. Apparently, there are several known viruses that attack the brain and the worst one known to the doctors is the herpes virus. This is what they were treating Rachel for.

John and I went for a cup of tea and came back to sit outside intensive care for what seemed like hours. We were so anxious to be with Rachel and a little frightened in case she was awake and wondering where we were. Eventually we were brought in to her and what a shock we got. There was our little Rachel in this huge bed, connected up to so many tubes and machines. It was like something out of ER. A few years previous to this we had seen John's father in an intensive care unit after a serious operation, but he was a big man – it was so awful to see the size of little Rachel with the tube from the ventilator coming from her mouth. We went each side of her and the nurses explained everything they had done. After they inserted the ventilator they had to do a chest X-ray to make sure everything was in place. She was connected to a lot of different monitors, all bleeping away and sometimes alarms would go off – we got used to these after a while. She had a lot of different tubes coming from her going into various bags and drips inserted in both hands. After a while we looked around. It was a very modern unit and everything bright and clean. There were about four other beds, but as far as I could see Rachel was the only child.

At this stage the various blood tests were coming back and everything appeared normal. The only one that showed anything unusual was the monospot test, which proved she was positive for glandular fever. Now, I hadn't a clue what the monospot test was, but they seemed to be clinging on to this. I asked a nurse what it meant and I was told that kids can get glandular fever, sometimes after chickenpox, or just out of the blue. It takes a long time to go away and the person who has it is tired all the time. So I thought about this for a while and hoped that this was what it was. I was already making plans for Rachel when she came home and I reckoned that even if she had to miss out on time at school, she could always repeat a year. I didn't have too much time to dwell on this as they quickly decided that there was more to it than glandular fever. Apparently, as I have found out since, just because a person tests positive it doesn't mean that they actually have it. Someone mentioned that it was contagious so I was on to my doctor and made him come out to the house and take blood tests from the other three. I was in a bit of a panic of course, but I felt I had to be doing something and I was scared that the others might get whatever Rachel had.

At this stage it was Sunday evening 31 October, and it had been such a long day. Rachel's X-ray on her chest showed that she had pneumonia. I was in an awful way – here we were in intensive care with Rachel, being told that she could well have something called encephalitis, that she had glandular fever, that she had pneumonia and that throughout all this she was still having the seizures. She was so sedated by the Medazalin that she was totally out of it, but we still talked to her and held her hands. We were told that she would be left on this medication for twenty-four hours and then they would start weaning her off. By then the seizures should have stopped or least be controlled. John went home as planned and I prepared for the night. I wasn't allowed to sleep in the Intensive Care Unit, but there was a little waiting room nearby where I planned to rest on the couch at some stage.

Even though the ICU is not a very nice place to be, there is a very 'safe' feeling there – I suppose that is because each patient has his or her own nurse twenty-four hours and it is so quiet and peaceful. That's not really true as there are so many monitors bleeping, but still, it is so different from a normal ward. We weren't there for too long and yet I got to know the nurses so well. They were all so concerned for Rachel and her beauty affected all of them, even though she couldn't talk or open her eyes.

At this stage Rachel was very heavily sedated, but she still had ongoing slight facial seizures. I learned to recognise the signs immediately. They never lasted long and sometimes you wouldn't even notice them. At some hour of the night, I left her and went out to my couch – it was so quiet out there and I tried to get some sleep as I knew there was another long day to follow. It was hard to settle with so many things going on in my head. I was worried and knew that whatever was wrong with Rachel wasn't something straightforward. I felt very lonely and wished John was with me, but at the same time I was comforted by the fact that he was at home with the others. I dozed off and woke around six and went straight down to ICU, praying that there would be an improvement. The nurses told me that Rachel continued to have the slight seizures and that we would have to wait and see what happened during the day when the Medazalin would be reduced

I sat with Rachel all morning and talked to her and told her everything that was going on. I don't know whether or not she could hear me. Because of her pneumonia, her lungs had to be suctioned on a regular basis to get up the secretions that were lodging there.

As soon as they got one clear, the other one filled up. There were so many 'jobs' to be done and she really kept her nurses busy, checking her temperature, gases, pulse, heart beat and medication.

I was thinking about the kids at home, back at school after the break, and I could imagine them talking about Rachel and wondering when she would be back. So many times during that terrible time, I kept thinking 'If only we were all back at home and everything back to normal.' Sometimes I couldn't actually believe that all this was happening and would hope that it was all a bad dream and that I would wake up any minute.

During the day John came in and the doctor seemed to be pleased with Rachel's progress. She seemed to be more alert and squeezed our hands in response to us. They started to reduce the Medazalin, her seizures had stopped and she was definitely becoming very alert. We were becoming concerned about how she would react if she woke up fully and realised she was on the ventilator – I was fairly sure the first thing she would do would be to try and pull the tube from her mouth. The doctor agreed that if she continued to improve the ventilator could be removed. We were so excited and kept talking to Rachel and telling her she was doing great and would be back to normal in no time. As we predicted, as the drug was reduced, she started to put her hand to the tube – she felt uncomfortable and was trying to do something about it. It was agreed to take her off the ventilator so we were asked to leave and wait outside while this was being done. We were so happy and hopeful and didn't mind how long we had to wait outside that door.

When we next saw Rachel, she looked just fantastic without that tube stuck down her throat. She still wasn't completely awake and we knew we would have to have patience. At this stage it was Monday afternoon and this lady came to do a test called an EEG – she had a big machine with a monitor and she had to attach several electrodes to Rachel's head by using a sort of glue, which we were very put out about. We started telling her not to ruin Rachel's hair with this glue stuff and we told her how proud Rachel was about her hair and how we hoped that the glue would come off easily. While this was being done there was a lot of activity around Rachel's bed, but we were still allowed to stay and we noticed that she was starting to wake up. She opened her eyes and looked at me and asked, 'Where am I?' I told her where she was and what was happening and then she asked 'Where are you?' and I told her that Daddy and I were with her and she was nearly better and we would all be going home soon. We were so thrilled – I was nearly crying with joy.

Those were the last words she ever spoke. Shortly after that, she turned her head and the stare came in her eyes and we all knew another dreaded seizure was coming. I nearly cried again, this time with disappointment. How could this be happening, just when we had our hopes up so high? So the seizures returned; the ventilator had to be inserted again, as she was put back on the strong medication and we had to wait outside while all this was being done. We both felt so low and down and just didn't know what to expect from that time on.

I went home that night and John stayed. Once again the phone never stopped ringing. People called and I just didn't know what to tell them. We didn't understand what was going on, or what was going to happen with Rachel. I tried to be cheerful with Laura and Bernard and Liam, but I couldn't really hide my worries from them. I spoke with John every hour – things were much the same. The following morning I called up to the school and explained to the teachers what was happening. I was worried in case Bernard might get into trouble if he didn't have his homework done. They assured me not be worrying about things like that and said they would all pray for us. Everyone was very good and I knew we had the support and prayers of everyone at home. At this stage we knew that we would be coming and going for a while so Irene said she would stay at the house until we were back to normal. Irene has been like a part of our family since the kids were small, and I was comforted knowing that she was taking charge of things at home.

When I got back to the house John rang to say Rachel's doctor had made some enquiries, and had got her a bed in Temple Street Hospital in Dublin under a very good neurologist, Dr Lynch. In Limerick, they said that they had done everything in their power, but the seizures weren't in control and Rachel was still quite sick. They thought that Temple Street might be better able to cope as they specialise in children and this Dr Lynch had an excellent reputation. So I was shocked but relieved that something was being done and felt hopeful and also a little frightened.

I packed some extra things for myself and John and as I was leaving a friend called and asked me how long I would stay in Dublin and I told her as long as it takes – I said I would stay until we would all be coming back together!

When I got to the hospital there was a lot of activity and we learned that we were very lucky that this bed in the ICU had become available. We were also told that I wouldn't be able to travel in the ambulance, as there wouldn't be room. It was an emergency ambulance, with two drivers, a doctor, an anaesthetist, a nurse and an awful lot of equipment. John and I said we would drive behind the ambulance.

It took about four hours to get Rachel ready and we watched it all. The two ambulance drivers waited with us in the ICU while we watched them preparing transfer sheets, emergency equipment if needed and, of course, the oxygen as she was to be kept on the ventilator. While they were doing this, one of her lungs collapsed and it took a while to stabilise that. Each time we thought we were ready to go something else had to be checked and rechecked. Every possibility was covered. I had tears in my eyes as I watched them wrap her up like a package on this high trolley with bottles and drips and bags hanging off it. I wanted to take her and wrap her in my own arms and run away with her. I was so scared and frightened and actually hated leaving the safe clean ICU.

At long last she was ready and they took her out to the ambulance. I gave her a kiss and wished her a safe journey. We had intended following them on behind them in the car, however, we hadn't even left the car park when the ambulance had disappeared from view. It tore off at high speed with flashing lights and a Garda escort to get them out of the city as fast as possible. Apparently, they wanted Rachel to be in the ambulance as short a time as possible in case anything went wrong. At this stage we didn't know whether Rachel was in danger or not, but we were very anxious and frightened and at the same time hopeful that things would be all different once we got to Dublin. Even though I would have liked to have been with Rachel in the ambulance, I was glad I was with John as it wouldn't have been nice to do that journey alone and we talked and told each other our fears and worries and our hopes. We made some calls and let everyone know what was happening.

Somewhere outside Dublin we pulled in and rang Temple Street to see if they had arrived and, thank God, they had. Rachel was being settled in to her new accommodation and the nurse said it would take a while, so told us not to rush. We had something to eat as we didn't know when we would get a chance again and neither of us could remember when we had eaten last, but we knew that this was going to be a long haul and we needed to keep our strength up for each other and for Rachel.

Rachel's Stay In Dublin

Around 8 o'clock we got to Dublin. Now John and I have been to Dublin on numerous occasions yet we still find it hard to find places so we had some difficulty finding Temple Street. Eventually we found the hospital – we had actually driven by it twice and not realised that it was a hospital. We found a place to park, went up to the front door and, to our dismay, found it locked. We then went down a side entrance and found an open door and got a bit of a shock when we walked in. It wasn't what we had expected and it was definitely very different from the modern unit we had just left behind us in Limerick. Temple Street Hospital was originally an old convent that had been converted to a hospital, so the layout wasn't very practical. There were lots of narrow corridors and winding stairs. As I said, our first impressions weren't great and we looked at each other and said 'What have we done?' However, after only a couple of hours there we changed our minds and found it to be the most homely place with lovely, caring staff who were so good to us and to Rachel. I think the fact that we were so tired and worried and frightened that night didn't help the situation and we were in a better frame of mind about the hospital the following morning.

That first night, we followed directions upstairs to intensive care. Halfway up the narrow stairs, there was a little landing with a place to sit and an intercom where we had to buzz and say who we were and then we would be told whether we could go up or not. The ICU was very small with one general room and then one little room on its own for children who were in isolation. That's where Rachel was. Inside the main door there was a little sink – we had to wash our hands each time we went in and we had to put on disposable aprons. The first thing I noticed when I went in was how small everything was, and then I noticed all the photos on the door and the wall; they were pictures of kids who had been patients there and who had recovered. I planned to have one of Rachel up there too someday.

As we entered we were so excited to be seeing Rachel again. There were two nurses with her and we noticed straight away that the ventilator tube was up her nose and not in her mouth like it was in Limerick. The nurses explained that they always did this as they figured it would be more comfortable for Rachel. It took us a while to get used to the nurses as we had known all the nurses in Limerick so well. However, we soon got to know all their names and found them to be absolutely fantastic. They were all mad about Rachel and kept saying how beautiful she was and asking us loads of questions about her and the rest of the family. They spoke to Rachel all the time and were so gentle with her. They were still getting her organised and told us that it would be morning before Dr Lynch spoke with us. They were continuing with the same treatment that she had had in Limerick.

We stayed with Rachel and watched as the nurses made her as comfortable as possible. We were getting very familiar with the procedures now; the lungs being suctioned every so often, blood taken for testing, the different monitors, setting off alarms when something was wrong. We talked away to Rachel, telling her everything that was happening and assuring her that everything was being done to get her well again. We spoke about all the things we were looking forward to – we told her we were looking forward to her being at home and that she would be thrilled to bits to hear about all the fuss she caused.

Later on we went to see the person who organised the accommodation for the parents. We were taken to a small little room, which was to be our 'home' for the following two weeks. We were also given a key to the 'parents room', a small room with a couch, some chairs, a coffee table, a kettle and some cups, a place to get away and have a quiet cup of tea or to meet up with a doctor or visitor. Even though it was a nice little room, I grew to hate it with a passion and hope I never have to set foot in it again!

We took in our stuff and checked out the rest of the hospital, which, as I said, was quite small. There was a beautiful little chapel where I spent some time each day; it was very peaceful and quiet, and there were lovely little soft toys around the altar. There was a canteen where one could get tea, coffee, breakfast or lunch, which was convenient, but again, it's not a place I would like to revisit. It was for staff as well as for parents, so often you would see the nurses on their breaks, chatting and laughing away and at the same time you would see mothers and fathers whispering to each other about their sick child, usually worried like ourselves. I never had much of an appetite there and just remember having tea or coffee with currant scones.

We brought up our fold-up bed and quilt, which we had used in Limerick, but to be honest I don't think we ever got round to setting it up. The room was so small and usually we took it in turns to sleep and the times we were together we would cuddle up on the single bed and hold each other, sometimes crying, sometimes sharing our worried thoughts and sometimes just falling asleep from exhaustion.

That first night we got a couple of hours sleep and went down to the ICU at around six. Rachel looked the same and the nurses said she had passed a comfortable night. All this time she was still getting the seizures and Dr Lynch and his team were amazed that the strong dosage of Medazalin was not controlling them. They confirmed that Limerick had treated Rachel with the best medication for the worst known type of encephalitis, which is the herpes virus.

That evening we thought there was a little improvement. Rachel seemed to be more relaxed with longer periods between seizures. At times her eyes were open and even though she didn't actually respond to us, we were certain she knew we were there and we sat at each side and held her hands and talked and talked to her. We rubbed stuff on her mouth and lips to keep them moist and we rubbed her ankles and took the weight off them so she wouldn't get sores. We tried to keep her little room as tidy and organised as possible but it was so 'busy' all the time and the nurses had no sooner finished administering her medication when it was time to prepare more, or do the gases – there was always so much to be done and we tried to help out as much as possible. Every so often phone calls would come to reception for us, calls from the ICU in Limerick, our own doctor at home, relations in Dublin and our own family at home as they would be so anxious to hear what was happening. We tried to ring home as often as we could, but there were times when we just didn't want to leave Rachel and of course we couldn't have our mobiles on.

That evening, we went out to get some fresh air and found that we were within walking distance of the city centre, so we went to have a bit to eat, which was grand. Even though we hated being away from Rachel, it was good to get out from the hospital for a little while and the nurses had our number if anything happened. We always told them where we were in case there was any change at all. After we returned we spent another couple of hours with Rachel. Every time we went into her little room, we hoped that this time it would be different and that the crisis would be over and that she would know us and we would be able to hug her and take her home. We were disappointed each time, but always tried to be cheerful while we were with her, as we believed at all times that Rachel could hear us. We knew she was sedated heavily and we also knew that she could feel no pain, which was of some comfort to us.

One of our main worries was whether or not the frequent seizures were doing damage to her brain. We were told that the machine to monitor the brain frequencies would be brought up the following day, and we were anxious to know what that would prove.

Her pneumonia was also a cause for worry, but I reckoned if they sorted out everything else and got her off the ventilator, then the pneumonia would sort itself out. We kissed Rachel good night and once again made the nurses promise that they would send for us if there was any change at all.

Next morning, Thursday 4 November, Rachel's seizures were more frequent and her pneumonia was quite bad. When I mention the seizures, they were only facial and really slight. We would see them coming on – her face would stiffen and if her eyes were open they would go into a stare and her face would twitch for a few seconds or maybe up to a minute and then it would stop. We began monitoring them ourselves and passing the information on to the nurses. I can't describe the feeling we had each time we knew there was one coming on – we would pray that each seizure Rachel had would be her last one, but it never was. They just couldn't seem to control them.

At this stage we spoke about one of us going home for a night. It was a very hard decision to make as neither of us wanted to leave Rachel, but we had three other children to consider and I knew how hard it was on them at home without either of us there. The phone calls are OK for a while but we knew one of us had to go. I was also aware that the end of the month had come and gone without any accounts been done. This might seem a silly thing to worry about, but it was something that couldn't be ignored and I knew that as each day passed the backlog would be getting bigger and bigger. So eventually, I decided to get the train down to Limerick that evening. As the day went on Rachel did not make any improvement and, in fact, seemed to be getting more seizures than ever. Dr Lynch and his team spoke with us on several occasions and told us that the medication was being increased all the time in an effort to control the seizures. He told us about an option of giving her a drug to knock her out completely for forty-eight hours – like being under anaesthetic for an operation – the idea being to deaden her brain and then after the forty-eight hours, when she would 'wake up', the seizures would have stopped. Dr Lynch didn't seem to want to do this at this stage and, to be honest, we didn't like the sound of it but then again, we could only be guided by them. Everything was out of our control and we had to put our faith in the hospital and in God above!

It broke my heart to leave Rachel that evening – it felt like I was being torn in two. I wanted to stay with her, but I knew I had to go home. John promised me he would tell me every single thing that happened so I kissed her goodbye and went down to the taxi with tears rolling down my face. The train journey was so long and dreary and I was already regretting leaving John and Rachel, but when I got home I knew I had done the right thing. Laura and Bernard and Liam needed me too and they were so happy to see me. They too were frightened and worried and wanted to know when Rachel was coming home. Nuala – a social worker in Temple Street – had arrived in to us with beautiful presents for Laura, Bernard, and Liam. I couldn't believe it and was touched by this lovely gesture. I took these presents home with me and of course the kids were thrilled to bits. It was lovely putting Liam to bed – doing something normal, reading him his story and telling him I would be there in the morning too. I got a lot of calls and tried to fill everyone in on what was happening. Loads of get well cards, Mass cards, and gifts had been left in for us and for Rachel and so many people were praying for us, which meant so much to me.

The news from Dublin wasn't so good. Rachel was having a very hard time. John rang me every hour and sometimes, when I would be out of my mind with worry, I would ring through to the ICU and talk to one of the nurses. It was the most terrible feeling to have Rachel so sick and her right across the country from me. I felt so lonely and so far away and several times throughout the night considered getting into the car and driving straight up. I got into bed, but didn't sleep. John, too, was having a sleepless night in Dublin. All kinds of thoughts went through my mind that night. I think this was the first time that I realised things were very serious and the fact that it was the middle of the night and John wasn't with me made it all the worse. I thought morning would never come. Liam came into me for a cuddle at some stage and I was glad of his company.

Things seemed to be a little better in the morning as they always do. They had managed to stabilise her and I calmed down a bit. I took Bernard up to school and went and spoke with the teachers, who were all so concerned and anxious about Rachel. I went down to the office then and tore into the accounts. I told the girls that I didn't want to take any calls apart from John and I didn't want to see anyone. I was determined to get the work done as fast as possible and I knew this wouldn't happen with interruptions. So I got the accounts done, closed down the end of month so the girls could continue, sorted the wages and was satisfied that evening that I had covered a lot. I knew I could go back up Dublin the following morning and that things were in control, thanks to our excellent staff and, of course, family. I spent a couple of hours with the kids and intended getting some sleep as I had a feeling that the next few days would be tough.

I spoke with John who was really having a tough time on his own. We both found it so hard when we were apart but realised that that had to be the way at times. He started to write things down in a notebook, which I am referring back to now. He found this helped him a bit. John is a person who is usually totally in control and found it very hard to accept that this was a situation where he had absolutely no control and there was nothing he could do to help his little daughter.

He told me that on the Thursday night they made a decision to put a 'main line' into Rachel's neck. This was instead of all the other smaller ones that were starting to cause problems. So this drip had several extensions off it and everything was inserted through this. That night they also increased the mixture of Medazalin and Epelim and for a while Rachel was seizure free and seemed very peaceful. John told me they changed her mattress – it was a bit like a water bed – very soft and bouncy; apparently these are used in cases where they don't want to disturb the patient too much and it prevents sores. Later on that night Rachel became fairly lively and alert; not awake, but moving her hands and legs and actually trying to take the tube from her mouth. John was thrilled to see this of course and they decided, rather than drugging her more, to strap her hands slightly so she wouldn't be able to pull the tube. During this time she squeezed John's hands and definitely seemed to respond to him.

However this was not to last. The dreaded seizures returned; at first very slight with long gaps in between, and then more frequent. They were only facial, but there all the same. John noticed that the seizures came each time the nurses were finished with her, taking the bloods for gases, or suctioning her. The following day Dr Lynch spoke to John and said he thought that Rachel was at her turning point. He said it would not be a good idea to take her off the Medazalin at this stage, but to leave her on it over the weekend and to start weaning her off it on Monday. If things were no better at that stage then he would have to seriously think about putting her on the drug to knock her out completely for forty-eight hours. We hoped that this would not have to be done. Dr Lynch said that a lady doctor, Dr King, would be on duty for weekend instead of him and that he would see us on Monday. John was also told that the guy with the EEG machine would be coming shortly to monitor the movements of Rachel's brain.

When Jim came with the EEG machine and started wiring Rachel up to it, John told him our concerns about Rachel's hair – there was so much of this glue stuff in it already that it was impossible to brush or comb. Of course we were very silly to be worried about such things at that stage, but you have to remember that we were certain that Rachel would recover and we would have her home again, and we knew how proud she was of her lovely, long hair. Jim was just lovely and so gentle with her and told us he would sort out her hair afterwards. He showed John how to work the machine and how to record the seizures. At this stage John could see from the monitor before the seizure started so he would start recording by pressing a pad and record until the seizure was over. The seizures were really slight, sometimes so slight that they only registered on the monitor and you couldn't see them on her face at all.

John phoned me at home every hour telling me that the seizures were very frequent. They increased the Medazalin about four times that night until Rachel was getting much more than even an adult should be getting. She was so drugged that the ventilator was doing most of her breathing for her. This went on for most of the night and of course her pneumonia was still bad, so all in all it was Rachel's worst night so far.

Morning eventually came and I found myself on the train back to Dublin. I met a very nice woman who listened to my story and my fears and it shortened the journey for me. I got a taxi to the hospital and literally ran to the ICU. The situation looked slightly better as things often do in the morning. I was so glad to see John again and so glad to see Rachel and be able to hold her hand and I had a little cry with her first – with relief to be back – and then they told me that she had stabilised a bit since last night. I was shocked to see this big line going into her neck and, of course, she was rigged up to the machine with load of wires connected to her head, but I was so glad to be there and not the other side of the country.

Later that day Dr King asked to speak to us in the parents' room. She went over everything that had happened to Rachel and told us how seriously ill Rachel was. She told us that she and Dr Lynch's team had treated children with encephalitis before. Some of them had recovered completely; some of them had recovered, but had been left retarded in some way; and some of them had died. She told us there was a possibility that Rachel might not make it and if she did, she would not be the same Rachel we had before the illness.

Now, this was a total shock to us. Maybe somewhere at the back of our minds we realised that Rachel was in trouble, but this was the first time someone said the words – she might die! I thought for a minute I was going to choke or lose my breath. Dr King left us alone and we just cried and cried and cried. How on earth could this be happening to us? How could we have come to this stage where we might lose one of our children? We held each other for ages and then cried some more and then tried to talk – it was so hard to say the words. We didn't know what to do or how to cope. We didn't know whether we had the strength to go back to Rachel after hearing such news.

We tried to pull ourselves together and be positive and hopeful and hang on to the fact that Rachel was alive and if ever she needed us, she needed us now. We tried to believe that Dr King was just preparing us for the worst scenario. It didn't mean that she would die. We know that Dr Lynch still had plans for Monday with the Thiopentone and we hung on to that. We said to ourselves that Rachel just couldn't die and that was that! Things like that only happened to other people, not to us. We went to our room for a while and then we went to Rachel, but of course we were only there two minutes when both of us started to cry – it was the most incredible feeling, one we will never forget, to feel so helpless and out of control.

We left again, as we still believed that there was a possibility that Rachel could hear and, no matter what, we didn't want her to hear us crying. I think I rang Mammy and told her briefly what had happened and then couldn't say any more and hung up, which wasn't very fair but I couldn't help it. We went for a walk and tried to eat a bit and decided that whatever happened we would face it together and we would try and be strong for each other and for Rachel. So we put the negative factors to the back of our minds and tried to be positive and faced back up to the hospital and went straight up to Rachel. As usual, we sat each side of the bed and we held her hands and talked to her and told her all the news and about all the things we would do when we got her home. I'm sure that she squeezed my hand. I know it seems unlikely with all the medication she was on, but I also know I didn't imagine it – she

definitely squeezed it. Now maybe it wasn't a direct response to me
– maybe it was muscle spasms or something like that, but I like to
believe that it was Rachel reassuring me that everything would be
OK and that she knew we were there for her and for what lay
ahead.

The next morning I went to the chapel to say my prayers. I
prayed so hard, especially to Kathleen, John's mother. She had only
left us a year and a half earlier and she was just cracked about
Rachel. She knew how much she meant to me, so I reckoned that
Kathleen just couldn't let anything happen to Rachel. I begged her
for help; I begged God for help; I begged them all up there to make
Rachel better. We spent the rest of the day with Rachel, talking
away to her, helping out whenever we could and keeping an eye on
all the monitors and readings. At this stage we had given up trying
to put nighties or pyjamas on her, as it was too hard trying to get
them on and off. We had gone shopping one day and bought lots
of stuff that we thought might do – sizes two or three times bigger
than her own and tops with front openings, but it was easier for her
not to wear anything. I also got a hair conditioner to spray on her
hair and I used to try and comb it out little by little.

Her pneumonia was quite bad that day and she had to be
suctioned very often. I was able to do this myself sometimes. At
some stage Dr King called again and she seemed very happy with
Rachel. We were delighted, of course, but so afraid to be hopeful.
All we could do was wait and take each hour as it came and we were
fairly certain that Dr Lynch would make a decision the following
day when he returned. We went out as usual that evening and had
something to eat. It was good to get out of the hospital and to get
a bit of fresh air but we always found ourselves very anxious to get
back. By now, it was 7 November, and Dublin was preparing for
Christmas. A lot of the windows were already decorated and it was
heartbreaking to see the kids full of excitement and joy and us so
full of sorrow and worry. I used to say to John, 'Wouldn't be lovely
to have Laura, Rachel, Bernard and Liam up here walking around

Dublin looking into the shop windows, all ready for Christmas?' And John used to say that all he wanted was for the six of us to be around the fire at home and everything back to normal.

That evening while we sat with Rachel she squeezed my hand again – it was such a wonderful feeling when she did this. As I said before I am not certain if this was a direct response to me, but I encouraged her so much and we kept talking to her as if she could hear us. Every time we got any little bit of reaction at all we were so excited and thrilled.

For our family and friends at home this was all very difficult. They were all praying so hard and were so anxious to get any bit of news at all from Dublin. We would ring a couple of times each day and try to pass on whatever good things happened that day. Of course, these were getting fewer and fewer, but we tried to be positive; there was no point in ringing home full of doom and gloom so we tried to sound strong and hopeful. There was so much hope there all the time. Not one of us believed that things would go so wrong for us. Everyone thought we would be coming home with Rachel any day and if not that her brothers, sister and friends would be coming up to see her and all sorts of presents were being made for her at school and at home.

It is difficult to describe the way I felt at that particular stage. I know I was so frightened and worried for Rachel. I almost felt sick with fear that she might never recover from this terrible virus that was taking over her little body. I wanted to be brave and strong and tried to convince myself that things would turn out OK. Each time I went in to her I prayed that she would be awake and that she would recognise me and respond to me, but I was so disappointed every time. I hated to see her the way she was – it was all so wrong. Beautiful ten-year-old girls are not supposed to be lying in hospital beds, connected up to machines and tubes!

The morning of Monday, 8 November, was decision-making time. Dr Lynch examined Rachel and told us what we had been dreading to hear. He was going to put her on a drug called

Thiopentone for forty-eight hours – the idea being that the brain would be completely deadened and when she would be weaned off this drug after the two days, the seizures would have stopped or at least that was the plan. This is a type of drug used to anaesthetise a person undergoing surgery. We were very frightened by all this but we had no choice and had to be guided by the professionals and we were told Dr Lynch was the best so we prepared ourselves for two more days of waiting. After all Rachel was completely out of it up to this, but we still felt very frightened and worried.

By 4 o'clock that evening she was completely knocked out, with only straight lines showing on the monitor. All we wanted was for Rachel to recover, but we were so amazed at the amount of medication being pumped into her and she so small on the bed – we worried how her little body could possibly cope with it all.

Up to this point Rachel was still in isolation, with no one allowed in to see her apart from us. My mother wanted to come up to be with me for a while, even if she couldn't see Rachel, but as it turned out, the nurses said it was OK and Mammy made plans to come up on the Monday by train from Mayo. When she arrived she was very shocked to see her little granddaughter in such a state.

It was great to see her, but I couldn't relax away from Rachel and there wasn't room for all of us in her room, so Mammy spent most of the day in the little chapel saying her prayers. She was able to pray much better than me as I found it so hard to concentrate. At this stage I had lots of little novenas and prayers that people had sent me, but as I say, I used to be so worried that I would end up crying or just rushing back to Rachel. Mammy stayed the night with her brother in Dún Laoghaire and spent some of the following day with us as well, which was great.

We went to get a couple of hours sleep and John decided to head home in the morning as we figured that it would be the following day before they would start weaning her off the Thiopentone. As we had planned earlier, one of us had to get home every couple of days to explain things to Laura, Bernard and Liam and to check all was OK at work. He decided to leave very early so I saw him off around 5.30 and went down to Rachel, who was still stable. When I say stable that was because the nurses kept increasing and decreasing certain drugs and monitoring her so closely – it was not an easy job, believe me. Mammy came out to me again and we had breakfast at the canteen and we chatted and she came into Rachel for short little periods and again spent a lot of the time in the chapel.

At home, a prayer meeting was organised at the church by some neighbours and friends and there was a huge gathering, all praying for Rachel's recovery. I was so touched by this and it meant an awful lot to me. The kids at school were also busy praying and I think there were candles lighting for Rachel in nearly every house in the parish. Only a person who spends time with their sick child in hospital would understand what something like this means to them.

All that Tuesday there never seemed to be a time when they were happy with Rachel – they were constantly meeting and talking and sometimes three or four of them would gather around and have a consultation and then they would go away and another three or four would come later. I knew they were worried and so was I. I rang John several times and kept him informed. He hated being away and I missed him so much and was twice as frightened and worried without him. However he had to go and he was due back in the morning and I knew I would definitely need him then when they planned to reduce the Thiopentone.

Rachel had gel pads on her eyes, I think to stop them drying out. She looked like someone from *Star Trek*. They attached some type of nebulizer to the respirator to help her breathing and also to help clear her chest. At some stage her temperature fell so low they had to wrap her in a tinfoil blanket for ages before it eventually came back up. Jim's machine was still on Rachel and he called in every now and again to keep an eye on it, but all that was showing was straight lines. However I did think there was a slight tremor on the lines each time I spoke to Rachel, so of course I made myself believe that was because Rachel could hear me and that was why the machine was registering same.

During the day an eye-doctor came to see Rachel. I hadn't heard anything about her eyes, so I was surprised. He examined her closely with his gadget, but he didn't say a word. The examination seemed to go on forever and I started to get very worried and frightened about the possibility of Rachel being blind. I thought about bringing her home blind and wondered how she would cope and how we all would cope. Eventually he finished and left and the nurses told me that her eyes were fine and I was so relieved that I cried. I think they were worried that the brain might be swollen and putting pressure on the optic nerve. I didn't question it further and of course so many other things happened after that there was no need to. Most of the time we felt that we had a great relationship with the nurses and doctors. They were so patient with us. However, at certain times – like the incident with the eye-doctor – we couldn't help wondering if they were keeping things from us, and this was very frustrating. We were constantly asking questions, but of course, those questions couldn't always be answered. So many times we were told that the next couple of hours would tell a lot, or to wait until the test results came back. It was like a waiting game. It was so difficult for us, but it was hard on the nurses too, as they couldn't tell us what we wanted to know. There were times when I felt like screaming, 'Do something! Sort Rachel out – now!' Unfortunately, that's not the way it goes.

When I think back I had so many different worries about Rachel during those two weeks that seemed so awful at the time, which just proves that we really had no idea what was going to happen.

That day Rachel had two sessions of physiotherapy and they left her on her side for some time. Sometimes they tilted the bed to bring her some relief. I still did my little jobs like lifting and rubbing her ankles, rubbing the gel on her mouth and lips and at this stage there was absolutely no point in trying to do anything with her hair – it was one big mess – a complete tangle. We bought a book for Rachel – *Ancient Fairy Tales from Ireland* – the stories were really funny, so I read several of them to her. The nurses had also brought us a tape-recorder and we had some of Rachel's tapes with her favourite music and we played them all the time. So, we had the Spice Girls and Britney Spears to keep us company! At first it made me very lonely to listen to these songs as it was only recently that Rachel and Laura and their friends had made up their own little dance routines to this music. I had some photos of Rachel in my bag and I put a couple of them up over her bed so the nurses could see what Rachel was really like. They were thrilled, and couldn't get over her lovely, long hair and beautiful smile. I remember that the first time I took out one of the photos it made John cry.

I took a break from Rachel and made all my phone calls. I spoke with the kids and with John who was coming back up the following morning. I rang a friend of mine in Dublin who came to the hospital and stayed with me for half an hour. When I got back to Rachel her temperature had risen sky high – I could see they were all worried, as they couldn't get it to come down. They got ice packs and put them all around her in the bed. I hated to see this happening. I was just shaking and so worried, frightened and lonely for John. It took ages and ages before the temperature started to come back down ever so slowly. Bloods were taken and I heard them talking about the fear of a new infection. While the bloods were being taken, the main line failed and a guy from theatre had to be called in to put in a new one. Now I was sitting right beside Rachel and this fellow asked me to leave without explaining to me what was happening. It was only later the nurses told me. So naturally I got upset because I just wasn't sure what was going on and I didn't know whether or not Rachel was in more trouble than usual. Now normally the nurses were just excellent and were with me all the way, but during this particular incident, there was a bit of a panic and they were all too busy treating Rachel and working with the guy from theatre that they forgot about me.

So there I was on my little seat on the stairs, more worried than I ever was in my life before. I nearly rang John a couple of times, but if I did I knew I wouldn't have been able to talk – I would have just cried and he wouldn't have had a clue what was happening. So eventually they called me back up and they told me about the new line and that the panic was over. After the usual washing of hands and putting on my apron, when I turned the corner, I looked straight up at the machines to see what the readings were of heartbeat, pulse, gases, blood pressure and temp. Only after all that did I look at my little girl. It suddenly hit me – I realised what I had done and how dependent Rachel was on all these machines. The tears came and I couldn't stop – I cried and cried and almost became hysterical. Majella, one of the nurses, tried her best to calm me down. When I eventually could manage a few words I said to her that Rachel seemed dead to me and that only the machines were keeping her alive. She tried to reassure me and told me that that wasn't true and that Rachel's temperature scare had frightened me, and that because I was tired and John was away it was only natural that it would all get to me. I just couldn't stay with Rachel any longer, so I gave her a kiss and went to my room where I cried and cried and got myself into an awful state. I suppose that was the first time that I realised that this terrible nightmare might not have a happy ending after all. I begged God for some good news in the morning and couldn't wait for John to come back. I pity any single parent who has to go through what we went through!

I slept for a while and when I woke up, my first thoughts were of how important this day would be for Rachel. I prayed again to God and the Virgin Mary and Kathleen to help her cope while the thyopentane was being reduced. I went down to Rachel at 6.30 and things seemed much calmer than the previous night. Majella said they had increased her blood pressure drug to keep things stable and put pads on her ankles to prevent sores as they wanted to move her as little as possible. I apologised to Majella for my behaviour the previous night, but of course she had seen it all before and told me

I had every right to act the way I had. While the changeover was taking place, I went to chapel to say my prayers and had a bit of breakfast at canteen and rang John who said he would be up before eleven.

I went back to Rachel at 8.45 and stayed with her until John came. At 10.30 they started reducing the Thiopentone from 13 mls to 12, and eventually down to 6 when they said they would leave it at that for a while. There were lots of problems keeping her stable during this time, so it was like we were holding our breath. This drug is quite strong and we learned that it takes a long time for it to leave the system, so we realised that the reactions we were waiting for would be slow. Her chest was still so bad and she was just about able for physio. It seemed awful to put her through this ordeal but without it she had no hope.

As the day went on we realised that it would be the following day before we knew for sure whether it worked. We talked so much to Rachel and held her hands. We read her stories and played her music and waited. One of the stories was so far fetched and funny and John and I had such a laugh over it – we knew Rachel would have laughed too. By that night (Wednesday) all drugs were reduced to very low levels, so we knew the following morning would tell a lot. Once again, we left her to get a couple of hours sleep and was so glad to have John back and felt much more hopeful and positive than the previous night.

The Beginning Of The End

The following day was Thursday 11 November, two weeks exactly after Rachel was first admitted to Limerick. We headed down to her as usual, our hearts thumping, not knowing what to expect, but trying our best to be positive. We did actually feel quite positive that morning. I can't explain it, but for an hour or two we chatted away to Rachel and kept telling her she was on the way to recovery – this was her day – soon she would be waking up and talking to us and we would be filling her in on all that happened for the two previous weeks. This kept us going and it was like the more we said the more we believed it ourselves. We also noticed that each time we spoke the lines on the monitor quivered, so we convinced ourselves that she could hear us and that her brain was responding. Even Majella was getting excited with us.

We took our usual break while the nurses were changing over and after the canteen, I went to the chapel and John went to make a few calls. We said we would meet back with Rachel so I was actually back first. One of the nurses told me that Dr Lynch was on the way, so I went up and called John and we sat with Rachel and waited. Within a few minutes the doctor came in with his team and started examining Rachel. We stood back and watched. He didn't do much, really, and he didn't say anything. He pulled back her eyelids and looked at each of her eyes. I didn't say anything, but I saw what he saw – I saw her eyes – no shine, no gloss – just dry eyes. He then tore off a bit of tissue paper from over the sink, a tiny corner of tissue, and he brushed this little bit of paper across Rachel's eye and there was no reaction whatsoever – nothing. That is all he did. Then he looked at us and said we would go to the parents' room to talk.

We didn't say anything to each other, just held hands as we walked to that room. We got to the room a few minutes before Dr Lynch and the nurse. I looked at John and said, 'This is going to be bad.' I kept seeing those lifeless little eyes before me. He said 'No' – he still felt a little of the excitement we had felt earlier that morning and did his very best to sound strong and hopeful. I started to get an awful, sick feeling inside me, and my heart was beating so loudly. At last they came and we all sat down. Dr Lynch started off talking about Rachel when she first came to the hospital and how they had treated her. I think he spoke for a few minutes and then got to the point where he said that our little girl was seriously ill. He explained about what they had done for the previous forty-eight hours and told us how he had examined her the previous morning and had seen no light in her eyes, but said he would give her another twenty-four hours when the drugs would be reduced, but that there was no change. He said there was nothing that could be done for Rachel. Her brain was dead. The machine was breathing for her and keeping her alive.

At this stage it is all a bit of a daze, but I think I took a breath and put one hand over my mouth to stop myself from crying or screaming or whatever I might have done and I think I held John with my other hand. I didn't take in anything else the doctor said, but apparently he spoke about the machine being turned off and then he left and I think the nurse spoke to us, but I really don't remember. She left us alone and the two of us were in total shock. Never did we really think this would happen. We knew things were bad, but nothing could have prepared us for this. We were stunned. We couldn't say anything for ages. Eventually I let out my breath and the tears came flooding down my face and John's tears came flooding down his face and all we could say was, 'No! No! No! No!

This could not be happening to us – Rachel cannot die – our little girl cannot leave us – something will happen to change things – the doctor is wrong!'

Deep down we knew the machines were keeping Rachel alive and we knew that Rachel was already gone from us. We knew that nothing would change and that there was no hope for her. Dr Lynch said that the following morning they would do some final basic tests to make absolute certain that her brain was dead and incapable of the most basic function, like breathing. A life support machine cannot ever be turned off until these tests are done.

So, I think at that stage we made our way to our room and tried to straighten ourselves and get our heads around everything. We had no idea what to do or where to turn. We both felt like screaming our heads off, or knocking our heads off the walls, but we sat down together and between the crying and the sobbing eventually came up with two facts; firstly, we needed someone to help us cope, and secondly, we had to figure out a way to tell Laura, Bernard and Liam.

We both knew that we would have to break the news to them ourselves – that they couldn't possibly hear it from anyone else. We also knew that it was impossible for either of us to head down to Clare or to talk to them on the phone. So we rang John's sister and told her to take the kids from school and bring them up to us. Bernard's birthday was coming up on the Sunday and the plan was that they would be told that I couldn't make it down for that, so instead they would come up to me for the weekend. Beatrice and her father collected Laura from Spanish Point, Bernard from national school and Liam from home, without letting on to anyone what was happening and they were all excited to be heading up to Dublin to see their Mammy and Daddy and Rachel.

Once that call was made we concentrated on our next problem. I knew straight away who I wanted with us and that was my first cousin, Fr Aquinas, who was based in Dublin. I knew that he had worked in Crumlin Hospital for sick children for years and I figured he would be able to help us if anyone could. I rang my mother, told her what was happening – I think I had to hand the phone over to John as I got completely choked up, and eventually got Aquinas' mobile number from her. I rang him and he said he would come straight out to Temple Street. He had known our situation during the previous two weeks and had been in touch with us. Then we cried some more and wondered where on earth we were going to get the strength to get through the following few days, and in fact the rest of our lives. I think our main dread at that time was facing Laura and the boys – how were we going to tell them? Why did we have to put them through this? How had our situation come to this?

Then I thought of something else and I couldn't bring myself to say it to John – every time I tried to tell him, the words would not come out – it was like this conversation should not be taking place. What I was thinking was whether we should talk to someone about Rachel's organs being donated. I eventually put it into words and John agreed with me that if it was possible we would let them use or take anything that might help someone else, especially if it gave life to someone else.

At this stage we were conscious of the fact that we should be down with Rachel – to spend whatever time we had left with her. We felt so shaken and weak and frightened and angry and lonely and frustrated and sad! I think Nuala, the social worker, and Sr Anne, came to us around that time. I don't remember the exact sequence of events as they occurred.

We did go down to Rachel. We sat each side of her bed and each of us held her hands. The nurses were administering her medication and drugs as usual, still taking blood for gases, still working as hard as ever. Jim was gone with his machine. He had given us a wave earlier through the window. Of course, we didn't realise at the time that he probably couldn't say a proper goodbye to us as he was actually taking away the machine at that time and probably knew that he wouldn't be needed any more.

When we sat down, neither of us could hold back the sobbing and the tears. We cried and cried. Then each of us in turn spoke to Rachel. We told her everything that was happening. We told her that she wasn't going to be with us for much longer. We told her that everything had been done to save her, but they couldn't do any more. We told her how much we loved her since the day she was born and that we would never stop loving her. We explained that Laura, Bernard and Liam were on their way up to say goodbye to her and that we would probably be bringing her home the following day. We didn't hold back anything. Each of us said everything that was on our minds and in our hearts and we even tried to have a laugh with her over special memories. Sometimes John would break down completely and I would go over to him and other times, it would be my turn and he would come over to me. We tried to console each other; we tried to tell Rachel everything while we had time; we hoped for a miracle, but really we knew that the machines were keeping her alive and that she was already gone from us. It was like a scene from a television programme, something that was happening to someone else. At times I hoped it was all a bad dream and that I would wake up soon and everything would be back to normal.

We stayed with Rachel all afternoon. We kept in touch with Beatrice and the kids who were on the way up. Fr Aquinas came and we met him in the parents room. When I heard he was there, my first reaction was that he would make everything OK. He would know what to do. As I have learned since, priests are only human like ourselves, and they cannot wave a magic wand to make everything all right. However, it was lovely to see him there. He is a very special person and it made me feel a little safe to have him with us. He said our decision to have the kids brought up to the hospital was a good one. We didn't know whether they should see Rachel the way she was or if they should remember her the way she was before she got sick. Aquinas told us to wait until we had broken the news to them first and then see what they wanted to do themselves. We reckoned that Laura and Bernard would definitely want to see her and that Liam might be better off sticking to his own memories of her. At no stage did we mention any actual arrangements regarding the funeral or getting Rachel home or anything like that. As far as I was concerned Rachel was alive, and I couldn't bring myself to even think of those details. Then something else dawned on me and I started to panic. Rachel was never confirmed – how could she die without being confirmed? Aquinas calmed me down and said that he would confirm her. Sr Ann got whatever was needed and Aquinas asked me what name I would like her to take for her confirmation. I didn't know what to choose, so I gave her my own name – Rita. We went down to Rachel – myself, John, Aquinas, Nuala and Sr Anne. And so Rachel was confirmed – nothing like the day Laura was confirmed eight months previously in Mullagh. Aquinas blessed her and said prayers – John and I cried through all of it.

By now Beatrice, Willie and the kids were in Dublin. We had organised for them to stay in a hotel and the two of us got a taxi and met them there. Our hearts were thumping – both of us trying to figure out how we were going to tell them, especially Laura. When we got to the hotel, they were in their rooms. Their faces lit up when they saw us – so full of excitement! Liam was running around the place and telling me he was going to make me a cup of tea. Laura was sizing me up – she probably knew from my face that something was wrong, but didn't say anything at first. Bernard was thrilled at the fact that he was going to be spending his birthday in Dublin with us. Before long, Laura looked at me and asked me the dreaded question – 'Mam, how is Rachel?'

I sat down on the bed and John sat beside me. Laura and Bernard sat down opposite us on the other bed. I held Laura's hands. I tried to talk without my voice shaking, but there was such a big lump in my throat. I managed to tell them about the virus that had attacked Rachel's body and how the doctors had tried everything to make her better. I told them that the virus had travelled to Rachel's brain and that it had done so much damage to her brain that she couldn't breathe on her own or in fact do anything anymore and that the machines were keeping her alive. We told them that the doctor had told us that the machines would have to be turned off. Now, up to this point, this was the hardest thing I ever had to do in my entire life. I would have done anything not to have been in that situation – telling my sons and daughter that their sister was going to die. I felt a massive anger in me that I had to do this – that they had to go through this at such a young age. It wasn't fair!

Laura's reaction wasn't good. She screamed at me 'Is Rachel going to die?' I said that she was. She shouted out 'No, No, No!' – she kept screaming it over and over again. She said 'No, Mam! Rachel can't die, she just can't!'

At this stage, we were all crying and holding each other. It didn't seem to have registered with Liam, but I knew I would have plenty of time to go through things with him and explain what was happening in a way he would understand. Laura and Bernard did not hesitate when we asked them if they wanted to see Rachel that night. They wanted to get to her as soon as possible. They were so shocked – no more than ourselves, they never realised that things could get to this stage. They knew Rachel had been very sick, but things like this only happen to other families, not to us! Poor Laura couldn't take it in at all and I felt so helpless. I was having problems coming to terms with it myself, but to see the pain on her face and not able to do anything about it was something desperate.

We decided that John, Laura, Bernard and Willie and I would go to the hospital and Beatrice would stay with Liam. It wouldn't have done Liam any good to see Rachel the way she was and he was delighted with himself exploring the bedroom, making tea and looking forward to sleeping in a different place. It wasn't good for him to see all of us so upset and it was difficult for us to cope with what was happening, never mind explaining it to him. So, we got a taxi – all of us were so quiet. I held Laura and Bernard while they sobbed their hearts out. I knew this was going to be so hard, but they had to see Rachel. I tried my best to prepare them, but how do you prepare your daughter and son for the last time they would see their sister alive, and for saying goodbye to her?

We got to the hospital and went up the stairs and all sat down on the little seat on the landing and buzzed the intercom. One of the nurses came down to us and introduced herself to Laura and Bernard. She told them not to be upset when they saw Rachel and explained to them the way the ventilator worked. She also explained to them about the other machines and monitors and told them they could ask her any questions. We then went up and went through the regular routine of hand washing and putting on the aprons. And then we were all around Rachel's bed, filling up the little room. I noticed some changes immediately. They had made a huge effort in making Rachel look as nice as possible. I think the bedclothes were different. They had managed to find a little nightie for Rachel. Up to that we hadn't been able to get anything on her with all the tubes. Her feeding tube was gone – I think her little stomach couldn't cope with food so there was no point in continuing with that. Really, I suppose that her whole system was breaking down, knowing the end was near. Her hair looked a little better even though it was still badly matted. A photo of the four of them was on the pillow beside her face, one I had given the nurses earlier. Her little sunflower teddy, a gift she had received while in hospital, was on the other side of the pillow and I think there was music playing. I noticed all these things, but all Laura and Bernard and Willie could see was poor Rachel lying there, connected up to a machine that was breathing for her. At first no one could talk – we were all completely choked up. Laura and Bernard just stared, full of amazement and shock and sadness. We all cried.

Eventually I found my voice and told them that Rachel might be able to hear us and to talk to her. So we talked to each other and to Rachel and they rubbed her hands. I think Nuala was with us for a while and she was so nice to Laura and Bernard. I'm not sure how long we all stayed, but the time came when we had to call a taxi to take Willie and Laura and Bernard back to the hotel where they were staying the night. We decided we would ring them in the morning to let them know what was happening. So they had to say goodbye to Rachel, knowing the next time they would see her, she would not be the same. I can't remember every detail of that and I can't think of words to describe those last few minutes. We went down to reception and waved them off. I hated leaving Laura – I wanted to be with her and hold her and make everything right, but everything was so wrong and I had to stay at the hospital, so I knew she had to go with the others.

After they left, we felt so drained and exhausted and angry that we had to put them through such an awful ordeal. We headed back up to Rachel and talked and talked to her, telling her how much we loved her and that we would never stop. Later that evening, my two sisters, Mary and Teresa, arrived from Mayo. We all held each other; there were no words to do the situation justice. They came in to see Rachel and were so shocked to see their beautiful little niece, who, a couple of weeks previously would have been tearing around the place and up to every kind of devilment! We all cried together and then they too left to stay with friends and said they would come again in the morning.

We went to our room that night to make our last routine calls. I rang Niamh's Mother and told her that Niamh would have to get a new best friend. I rang my own mother and my friend and told them all that things were not good and it looked like the machines would have to be turned off the following day. I didn't spend long talking to anyone. I couldn't say much without bursting into tears. My eyes were sore. My stomach was sick and my heart was slowly breaking. Every now and then myself and John would just look at each other and ask, 'Is this really happening – how could it be?' We would hold each other and cry and then we would tell each other that we would have to be strong and face this together and help each other. We went down to Rachel again and spent a few more hours with her. The nurses were still working on her and they were so professional and yet so sensitive to us. A nursing career is a true vocation.

At some stage we went up and lay down on the bed for a couple of hours. We knew that whatever happened the following day we had tough times ahead. I'm not sure whether we slept or not. So much going on in our heads. I felt mine was going to explode. Around 5.30 we headed down to Rachel again, secretly hoping for a miracle but knowing that really wasn't going to happen. As I said earlier, the nurses were still administering her drugs and trying to stabilise her blood pressure and temp. The previous day they had to introduce a new drug – adrenaline – I can't actually remember what this was for but it was becoming increasingly difficult for them to keep her stable even with the help of the ventilator. I think myself all her organs were starting to protest – they weren't able to keep working, but with the help of the drugs she was struggling on.

Dr Lynch was due at 10 o'clock the next morning to do the final tests and then the decision would be made. We were getting to the stage when we knew the end was near and in one way we wanted it to be all over, but of course in another way we were savouring each moment we had with Rachel. Eventually he came and we were sent down to the parents' room. It wasn't long before he arrived with one of the nurses. He told us what we had been dreading to hear. The tests proved one hundred per cent that Rachel's brain was completely dead – that it couldn't perform the most basic function of the body, which is breathing. The machine would have to be turned off. The doctor was very patient with us, explaining everything to us in exact detail. We had asked him the previous day about donating her organs, but he told us that this wasn't possible as Rachel's virus was unknown and therefore there would be too much of a risk in passing on any of her organs. He told us that the donor clinic had thanked us for the offer. He also asked our permission for him to do a post-mortem on Rachel to help him and his team to find out more about the virus and maybe help other patients with encephalitis. We consented to this.

I was anxious about how the machine would actually be turned off and what would happen after. I had remembered seeing a programme on TV once where the relatives had to leave before the machines were turned off and so I was frightened about that. They explained it to us very well and even though we would be with Rachel until the very end, they would have to take her fairly soon to do the post-mortem. Once we were clear on what was happening, we were determined not to spend another night in the hospital and planned to take Rachel home with us that night. It takes a few hours for the post-mortem to take place, so that was putting the people involved under pressure. But we had had enough and we signed the consent form only on the basis that it would be done in time to take her home with us.

Once we knew for certain what was happening, we rang Beatrice and the kids and told them to go back down home and that we would see them later. I had awful sympathy for Laura especially facing that journey being so upset. I would have loved to have gone with her and held her all they way home, but I couldn't. My two sisters came out to us again and we went to the canteen for a cup of tea. I remember them saying how warm it was and I was shivering so badly that one of them had to give me jumper to put round my shoulders. This cold, shaky feeling was one that stayed with me for a long time to come.

We were told that the machine would be turned off at 2 o'clock and that Rachel would be ready to come with us between five and six that evening. Once that decision was made we went back to Rachel and sat with her. Now as you can imagine, we were in a terrible state, out heads full of so many thoughts. We were in a situation that we never thought we would be in and we found it very frightening – a feeling of such helplessness overcame us. We still didn't talk about what would happen after the machine was turned off. A bit like when I was pregnant with the kids – we would discuss the possible names briefly, but never too much until our babies were actually born and in our arms.

I remember from 1.30 onwards – I kept looking at my watch. Every minute was like an hour. I knew someone had to come up from theatre to do the 'job'. I kept listening for his footsteps, delighted each time when it wouldn't be him. In another way, I wanted everything to be over – I wanted to be home. I was so fed up of the hospital and the waiting. I didn't want to wait any longer when I knew nothing in this world would bring our Rachel back to us. It would have been different if there was some little bit of hope to keep us going, but we didn't have any and we knew the inevitable had to happen. Nuala and Sr Anne were with us most of the morning – I can't remember what they did or said but I know they were there. Sr Anne gave Rachel her last rites and I think we all prayed. John and I had said everything we wanted to say to our little girl and we were ready to let her go – if such a thing is possible.

Rachel Leaves Us

At 2 o'clock the man from theatre came. The two nurses who were on since morning were with us. As always, John and I sat each side of Rachel, both holding her hands. The first thing that happened is that one of the nurses starting switching off each of the drugs, one at a time. Then the ventilator itself was switched off. I could still hear it working. I could hear her heart beating. I placed my hand over her heart and felt it go thump, thump, thump, strong at first and then getting quieter and weaker. Then her lips started to turn blue. Then I thought she was gone and said so, and the nurse said 'No, not yet' – she could tell from the monitor. Then I took Rachel in my arms and John held both of us. And during those few minutes, Rachel left us and passed on to her new home. It didn't take long, just about four minutes. We laid her back on the bed. Someone took the tube from her nose and we were allowed to stay with her. No one rushed us – this was our time. I gathered up her little teddy and the few photos that were on the wall and said goodbye to Rachel, and one of the nurses and John helped me out of the intensive care unit for the last time and once again found ourselves in that dreaded parents' room. I think we were left alone for a while and we held each other and I really thought that our tears would never stop.

The next thing I remember we were back in our room and now it was time to make the arrangements that we had tried to put off for so long. I was in an awful way – I suppose you could call it some sort of hysteria. I told John that we would bring Rachel home ourselves. I told him I wanted a white coffin. I told him I wanted to bring her straight to the church. I had this idea of Rachel being so small and fitting into a little white coffin that I would be able to carry myself. Eventually John calmed me down a bit and I tried to listen to him. You see, I knew what was ahead of us after the experience of Kathleen's funeral a year and a half previous to this. I remembered the three days of constant handshaking and all that goes with it. I figured that there was no way I would be able to face this – now that Rachel was dead, I just wanted to get home and to get everything over with and to return to some sort of normal living. Of course I was wrong to think like this and John was absolutely fantastic – he made me realise that it was so important that Rachel get a good send off and that things had to be done the right way.

At first we didn't know what way Rachel would be when we got her back – we were worried about her hair. I was thinking I would have to get a little scarf or wide hairband to cover it as I reckoned no one would be able to get it to look any way right. At this stage we had no car in Dublin so we made the call to the undertaker to bring up a coffin and for Beatrice's husband, Ger, to bring up a car. I was told we couldn't get a white coffin at such short notice, so a regular one had to do. I think it was called a three-quarter sized one.

We knew immediately that we would be bringing Rachel home to our own house, like we did with Kathleen and we planned to bring her to the church the following evening and bury her after Mass on the Sunday – Bernard's eighth birthday. We confirmed the details so that they could be passed on to the priest, the local radio, paper and all involved. Before this, we had rung Laura and the boys, and our two families.

Nuala came and spoke with us and told us about Pat, the mortician. Apparently, he has worked in Temple Street for years, having lost a little boy himself at a young age. Nuala said he looked after all the children so well and was so gentle and sensitive with them. She asked us what we would like Rachel to wear. Would you believe my mind went completely blank? I tried to think what Rachel's favourite clothes were and all that would come into my mind were the fancy, little dresses that I used to put on her when she was small. I rang Laura who was surprised that I hadn't thought of the navy pedal-pushers and the blue, fleece top that Rachel persuaded me to order for her from one of the mail-order catalogues a month or two previously. She was so thrilled when I got them for her as it wasn't usual for me get them clothes this way, and she wore them every Saturday evening to Mass and again on Sunday. I felt so silly that this hadn't come to my own mind. For now I handed over some new underwear and socks and a red nightie that Rachel had never worn to Nuala. We had bought these things for her earlier on when we came to Dublin first, but of course she couldn't wear any of them.

Nuala suggested that we get away from the hospital for a couple of hours and get some fresh air. The time was going so slowly. We decided that we would go out for a while. There was nothing to be done until Rachel was ready. Nuala promised us she would ring John's mobile if she needed us. We walked down as far as the Ilac Centre. At this stage all the decorations were up for Christmas and everywhere was full of Christmas shoppers. The first thing I saw when I walked in was the crib, which was just set up. Children were singing carols somewhere. I looked around and felt like screaming my head off. How could everyone be going around looking so normal and happy? Did no one care about my Rachel who was lying dead up the road?

What would face us when we got back to the hospital? How would Laura and Bernard and Liam react? Where would we get the strength to get through the next few days? How would we cope with Christmas, Rachel's birthday, the others' birthdays? What would Laura do without her sister? What would Niamh do without her friend? How would poor little Liam get on without his playmate and how would Bernard's birthday go? I found it hard to take it all in and kept saying to myself that later, when I was on my own with no distractions, I would try and figure it all out and go back over the previous two weeks and see what had happened to bring us to this terrible situation.

We went in somewhere to eat, as we didn't know when we would get a chance to eat again and couldn't remember when we had eaten last. I looked at the dinner in front of me, but could only take a couple of mouthfuls. Next we found ourselves in Roches. I couldn't remember whether Laura and the boys had anything good to wear, so I picked out a jumper for each of them and I choose a little white top for Rachel to wear inside her blue fleece – my last time buying clothes for her. Before we headed back to the hospital I saw a beautiful hair band with little blue roses on it, so I got it, still not knowing what we were going to do with Rachel's hair.

Our hearts were so heavy as we made our way back to the hospital for the last time. Just as we got into reception we met Nuala who told us she had just been down with Rachel and Pat had been blow-drying her hair. She told us that he had it perfect. We couldn't believe it as we had thought this to be an impossible task. We went to our room and packed up our stuff and then lay down on the bed and waited for them to come for us. I think we dozed off for a few minutes and we woke up with a fright when the knock came at the door. Nuala was there with the nurse who was on duty that morning with Rachel. Apparently it was her duty to stay with Rachel until the end. We followed them down the corridor and downstairs. I didn't even know where they had Rachel but we found out there was a mortuary on the ground floor near the chapel.

This was a bit similar to preparing to meet Laura and the boys the previous evening, as again, we didn't know where we would get the strength to face this. My heart was beating so loudly, but I thought I was feeling strong enough until I went in that door and there was my Rachel, laid out on some sort of bed in her red nightie and her socks and her hair back to normal – shiny and brushed – but she was dead. I freaked out completely. I screamed out, 'No, No, No! That's not Rachel! That's not our little girl who we left a couple of hours ago!'

My first reaction was just awful. I hit the walls. I cried. I couldn't touch her. I wanted to curl up and die myself. Nuala and the nurse had left us alone with Rachel. John went straight over to her and rubbed her face and said, 'Isn't she beautiful?' I kept saying 'No!' – how could she be described as beautiful? As usual, John managed to calm me down a bit. It was amazing really, but I would have preferred if Rachel's hair was still matted and if she was connected up to all the tubes. I had sat with her for two weeks with very little reaction or response from her, but this was so different. Back then she was alive. Now she was dead. The difference between life and death was really brought home to me during those few minutes.

After a while, I went near her and touched her small finger. It was so cold and hard and stiff. At this stage, Rachel had been dead for five hours. This set me off again, but eventually curiosity got the better of me and I became braver. She seemed to be so long on the bed and my idea of her being put into a small, white coffin was out the window. Her chest seemed to be really high and her lips were slightly parted and she seemed to be smiling. I couldn't get over how cold and hard she was. Even by touching her nightie I could feel the cold coming through. I felt her head and found where they had opened her during the post-mortem, but this didn't bother me. I was amazed that there were no marks around her nose or mouth from the tubes. Her face was perfect, as was her hair – thanks to Pat, however he managed it. I noticed the little hole on the side of her neck where the main line had been inserted. I stared at her and stared at her and found it so hard to accept what was in front of my eyes. I looked around the room and they had it done lovely. There was music playing, candles lighting and lots of little teddy-bears and toys around the place. After a while the two of us sat down and Nuala came in with a large brown envelope and gave it to me. Inside it were a couple of things they had put together. First of all there was a little booklet especially done for us in memory of Rachel. Beautiful little prayers and sayings, Rachel's footprints and fingerprints and a little bit of her hair and her hospital wrist band.

Even though this brought a fresh flood of tears, I was very touched by the effort they had gone to and I knew this would always be very special to me. Next, there were two blue, laminated sheets. On one, there was a song called 'Rachel's Song' and on the other there was a piece called 'Rachel's Rainbow'. When I read the rainbow one I knew straight away that I would have this read out at Rachel's Mass – I knew that this was something I would read over and over again, and how right I was.

Then Pat came in and Nuala introduced us to him. What a lovely, quiet man who had done such a wonderful job on Rachel. He has such a difficult job, but one he does very well and we were touched by his efforts, as we know it must have been so hard to get Rachel's hair sorted.

We were surprised by what happened next. The door opened and several of the nurses came in to say good bye to Rachel. These were nurses who were on duty that day and during the previous two weeks. They were all crying and some of them were so emotional that they couldn't even speak to us. After they were gone, we could hear them in the next room, crying so hard and being consoled by Sr Anne and Nuala. This was a side to the nurses we hadn't seen before – they were always so professional, but it showed that they were only human too, and once again, we were touched. It also made me realise that John and I weren't the only ones affected by Rachel's death.

By now it was about 8 o'clock and we had heard that Ger and the hearse were delayed and it would be another couple of hours before they got to Dublin. We were comfortable with Rachel then and we told Nuala and Sr Anne and Pat to go on home, that we would be fine, but they wouldn't hear of it. While we waited, Sr Anne and Nuala spoke with us and told us lots of interesting things about themselves and their work, and Pat kept an eye out at the door making sure there was parking place for the hearse and the car. Nobody realises the true vocation and dedication that these special people have and we will be forever thankful to them.

I kept looking at Rachel like I had for the two weeks previously when I would be looking out for some change, but there was no point looking for a change now. She was so still. We found her watch and put it on and also her little Claddagh ring.

At last they came. During this whole episode, there were so many periods of waiting. So this particular time of waiting was over and the hearse was outside the door to bring Rachel home. I think there might have been a prayer, I'm not sure. The main thing I remember is Pat picking up Rachel and carrying her over to the open coffin they had just brought in. Rachel remained completely stiff and straight – I was so shocked. Normally when a child is picked up they go limp, but because Rachel was dead so long this didn't happen. I started crying again and when they put the lid on – I felt so empty.

Rachel's Last Journey

We put all our stuff in the car and I cuddled up on the back seat with the quilt on top of me. I had my mind made up that I would fall asleep and not wake up until we were home in Quilty. Unfortunately this did not happen. It was like my head was too full to fall asleep. I tried so hard, but I just couldn't block it all out. It was the longest journey of my life and every time I felt the car slow down and turn, I thought it was the turn up to the house and I would find out that we were only a couple of miles further that the last time I checked. However we eventually arrived back in Quilty. I'm not sure what time it was but it was very late and even though there had been people there earlier, most of them had gone home so it was a quiet house we faced. The kids were in bed. Rachel was taken in and I couldn't help remembering the night we left with her two weeks previously. Never in my wildest dreams did I think she would be coming home in a coffin.

They brought her into the dining room, which was all ready – the same way it was done the time Kathleen died. They took off the lid and there Rachel was, just the same, still dead, still cold and hard. The undertakers had to do their job then so I went upstairs and got the clothes that Laura had ready. I woke her gently and told her we were home, but told her to go back to sleep, which she did. I started looking for a polo neck then as I thought Rachel's neck should be covered on account of the little hole, but then decided that the polo neck I had was navy and it was too dark so I decided on the little white top I had bought earlier. I picked up her little, gold locket that we had given her the previous Christmas with photos of John and myself, and then I got the hair band and gave them all to the undertaker. He closed the door. This is something they do themselves, so we left it to him.

After an hour or so I came back downstairs and they were finished with Rachel. I got upset all over again when I saw her. The hair band looked beautiful on her and matched her fleece perfectly. Her hair was always nicer off her face. Her hands were joined with a little rosary that I had found upstairs – a gift for one of their Communions. The more beautiful she looked the worse it was for us to see her like that. There was about a foot of extra space from her feet to the end of the coffin so I put a teddy there to fill the space. I was really worried about Laura, Bernard and Liam's reaction to her and knew that I would have to go up and wake them soon.

I woke the boys first – they were so excited to see me and I was thrilled to be able to hug them. Of course their first question was where was Rachel so I tried to prepare them as best I could. I wanted to have a little time with them first so I took my time getting out their clothes and telling them that they had to be nice and clean and tidy for Rachel. We tried to talk about normal things and they told me what had been happening at school and with their friends. I knew once we went downstairs, things would not be normal for a while. By then Laura had woken and we held each other for so long and we both cried. Again, I did my best to describe the way Rachel looked and told her we would all go down together and we would have to be very strong. We couldn't put if off any longer so I took Liam up in my arms and the four of us went down together. Liam's reaction was much as I imagined – he just stared at Rachel and wouldn't touch her at first He said she looked like she was sleeping and after a few minutes he lost interest and ran around and started taking in the strange atmosphere in the house. Bernard, who is always curious about everything, did a lot of staring too and noticed every little thing about Rachel and asked me a lot of questions, which I answered as truthfully as I could. He cried a bit and then went off to get something to eat. I told them that Rachel would be there all day and they had plenty of time to get used to her and they could come and stand by the coffin whenever they wanted and if they had anything special that they wanted to put in with her, they could. This gave them something to think about.

Poor Laura – she cried and cried and cried and I couldn't console her. I think at this stage I was becoming a little stronger myself and my main worry was Laura. I just couldn't calm her – it was like she couldn't take it all in. I was so concerned, but just couldn't make it right. I think it was around 7 o'clock by now and some of my friends started coming. Everyone's reaction was the same – most couldn't say anything – they were just totally shocked and saddened.

The day went by very quickly. There was no plan for the day apart from the arrangement to bring Rachel to the church around 8 o'clock that evening. That seemed to be hours and hours away and we thought we had loads of time to organise ourselves. However, people started coming early and never stopped at any stage. The dining room, living room, kitchen and hallway were constantly full. Tea was being made in the kitchen. I was not aware of who was doing what, but we were surrounded by close family and friends at all times, and they were all fantastic. As I said my main concern was Laura and I was glad when some of her friends called in from time to time, but mostly she ended up back at my side and seemed to want to stay close to me. We mostly stayed next to Rachel. John was there too and the boys were taking advantage of the excitement. Liam was getting braver all the time and would stand up on the chair beside the coffin and say, 'Mam, can I kiss Rachel?' and I would lift him up and he would give her a kiss. After a while he could do this by himself and gave her so many kisses and was very comfortable with her.

The various people that came during that day caused different reactions in me. My heart nearly broke when Niamh and her family came. After all, herself and Rachel had been so close and had so many dreams and plans. For most of the children that came, this was their first experience of seeing a child laid out, so it was totally new for them. Niamh and Rachel used to play with twin dolls that Niamh had so she brought these, putting one in with Rachel and keeping the other one. She also wrote her a letter, and enclosed a locket with photos of both of them and placed these in the coffin too. All Rachel's other friends came too. Actually, all the children from her school came at some stage during the day. Each one brought fresh tears to my eyes, as I would have a particular memory of him or her with Rachel. Lots of them brought flowers, little gifts, teddy bears, letters, photos and all of these were put into the coffin. By the end of the evening, we were glad of the size of the coffin to fit in all this stuff which made Rachel look as if she was surrounded by love and affection, which she was. My own family came, my mother, my father, my brothers and sisters and their families; relations came from Dublin and England. Neighbours of my parents in Mayo came – people I hadn't seen in years, but who came to support us and to support Mammy and Daddy. I felt so awful when I saw the faces of my parents who had to see their little granddaughter in a coffin. They were grieving for the loss of Rachel, and also for me and John.

Rachel's dancing teacher came with a trophy, which we placed in the coffin. Rachel's schoolteachers came. Everybody came. Towards the evening, there was a constant queue and even though I knew every person and child that came, sometimes it was all a blur. My eyes were so sore and I was trying to console Laura and other kids, and trying to talk to people. Most of the time I found I just wanted it all to be over, and I didn't think I could cope with any more. Everyone was crying, even the men, but it was the little children who were most upset and I ended up trying to comfort them, but their tears kept coming. All that kept going on in my head was that if I had time alone and some silence I would be able to get my head around everything. I wanted to think about Rachel and about what happened to her, but I had to go through all this first. At the same time, I was deeply touched by the people who came and the comforting things they said to me. I was amazed at particular people who whispered to me that they understood, that they had been through the same thing, some of them, years and years earlier. These were people I knew, but I had never known that they had lost a child during their life.

Eventually 8 o'clock must have come because someone said it was time to say the rosary. John and I couldn't believe it was time to go. I expected that after the rosary everyone would leave and we would have a few quiet minutes with Rachel for each of us to say goodbye and I was dreading this moment. As it happened there were so many people in the house it was impossible to empty the room completely and everyone wanted to say goodbye over and over again. Poor Rachel got so many kisses that at the end I had to hold her little face so it wouldn't be put out of place and before I realised it, it was my turn to give her my last kiss and the lid had to be put on. Sad as it was, I still had this feeling that I just wanted to get on to the next stage of this saga and we hurried everybody on. Anyway, I had already said my goodbyes to Rachel, several times.

I organised coats and jackets for everybody and the men got organised for carrying the coffin. Someone used to this situation took charge. Apparently there is either a tradition or routine for this – the way the uncles and relations offered to do it and turns had to be taken. Rachel was going to be held high all the way back to the church. We had done this with Kathleen too. I've heard since that there were loads of people outside on the driveway and on the road. There were Guards of Honour with all the kids from the school in their uniforms, the ladies football club and the Lahinch swimming club. She really did get an excellent send-off. Not that I noticed much of it on that night. I was just concentrating on getting this over with and concentrating on keeping Laura, Liam and Bernard close to me and assuring them everything would be all right, which was stupid because I knew that wasn't true.

So, we all walked behind Rachel, everybody crying. We got to the church and the priests were waiting for us. All the beautiful flowers and wreaths were brought in and left around Rachel. Fr Tuohy spoke and what he said was beautiful. He called her 'little Rachel' – this is what he used to call her when she served Mass. I can't recall exactly what he said, but I know I was very touched and appreciated his words. After the prayers were said and the priests had left the altar, the people started coming to offer their sympathy. Now, I know this is tradition and the right thing to do, but I found it so hard. I know people mean well and they care, but there were so many and it took so long and just like during the day there were certain people who sparked off certain memories and the fact that the majority of these people were so upset themselves, it was so difficult. Laura and the boys were wrecked and I wanted us all to be home. Earlier I thought about leaving Rachel in the church all night on her own, but strangely enough I didn't mind too much when we were leaving. Maybe I reckoned that she was in God's hands now and He would look after her. I couldn't think straight – I just wanted to get back home.

When we did get back to the house, it was full of people. Again, well-meaning family and friends were all so good to us and I appreciated their help and support. I looked around and everyone was having tea or drinks and chatting away. I felt like screaming and telling them all to go away. But this wouldn't have been the proper thing to do. I tried to make an effort and talk to people, but there seemed to be a lot to do. I wanted to get the kids to bed, as it had been such a long day. Some people were talking about the Mass and things had to be sorted regarding readings, prayers and gifts. Eventually most people left and we got the kids to bed and organised our clothes for the following day. I knew that the funeral Mass and Rachel's burial would probably be the hardest of all. I also knew that it would be an end to a certain stage and I would be able to do what I wanted to do for so long – sit down on my own and get my head around everything. I was so anxious to do this and I think the thoughts of it kept me going and kept me sane.

The following morning I went into Bernard's room early to wish him a happy birthday – what a day for a boy to have his eighth birthday! We gave him his Gameboy, which I had luckily got about three weeks previously. He was just thrilled and it was lovely to see him smiling and full of excitement. Laura was still very down and I tried to keep as close to her as I could. She wore the blue top I had got for her in Dublin and she was going over the reading that she was going to do at Mass.

There were a lot of people in the house that morning. Food was being organised for after the funeral. Thankfully I didn't have to worry about this – someone had taken charge and told me everything was under control. Everyone was so good and seemed so glad to be able to do something. We walked over to the church – there was no hurry, we knew our seat would be free. Once again so many people came, family and friends from far and near, all those that worked with us and so many customers. The children turned out in full force, from the schools, the swimming club and football club. Before we sat down I looked through the cards on the wreaths and again was touched by what was written on them and surprised at how many were there.

The Mass was beautiful. There were a lot of priests and the choir and the solo singers were fantastic. I cried a lot through it, especially when Laura and the kids did their readings and prayers, and when the gifts were brought up. Everything was so organised and it really was a special occasion. After the Mass was over, once again we had to go through the ritual of hand-shaking. I was amazed that there were still so many people waiting to offer their sympathies to us. I knew that their hearts went out to us and that they meant well but I found it so difficult. The high feeling I had during the Mass did not last very long.

Eventually it stopped and we had to do our last job – carry Rachel on her last journey to the graveyard. The men carried her

and we walked behind. John cried a lot. I think everyone was
crying. Each of the kids held a single rose. It was very lonesome
turning in to the graveyard. The prayers were said and the coffin
was lowered down. How many times had I said good bye to Rachel?
The single roses were thrown in on top of Rachel and the cover was
put on and all the beautiful flowers and wreaths were left on top. I
hated seeing Laura and the boys cry so much. I felt so cold and
empty as if a part of me had gone down into the cold earth with
Rachel. Actually the morning was beautiful for November – the sun
was shining, but I still felt so cold.

We spoke to people for a while and then headed back home.
Once again, everything was organised and suddenly the house was
full of people eating and drinking. I was OK for a while and spoke
with my relations, some of whom had travelled a long way to be
with us. We started looking at photos and only then realised how
important they were. I was always good with photos and had them
all over the place. I had loads framed on the walls and several full
albums of all the children since they were babies. I had a diary for
each of them as well and cried my eyes out when I looked at
Rachel's. At last, evening came and everyone left apart from a
couple of close friends. We sat around the fire and talked about
Rachel and I told them some funny stories. This was the nicest part
of the day. Then they left and it was just ourselves, the first time we
had a bit of peace and quiet and we were glad of it. We were drained
– no energy at all. We went to bed and hoped that by the next
morning we would feel a bit more refreshed.

Life Without Rachel

The following day I didn't go to work and the kids didn't go to school. However, I knew that the sooner we got back into some sort of routine the better. The more time I had with nothing to do, the more time I had to think. It was better, too, for Laura and Bernard to get back to school. When I did go back to the office, I couldn't face anyone at the counter and I couldn't take phone calls. I hid myself down at the back desk and the only thing that kept me going during those first couple of weeks was the post. Every morning I got cards and letters from family, friends, and people I had never even met. These meant so much to me. When the post arrived, I would put aside all the regular window-envelopes and make a pile of my own stuff. Some were just Mass cards, but the ones with personal notes or letters were the ones I read over and over again. I was amazed and surprised with this reaction from people and was deeply touched. My friends called to see me and I think I spent more time up in the kitchen drinking coffee than I did at my desk. If I wasn't in the kitchen, I was in with John, who was so worried about me.

During those first couple of weeks after Rachel left us, Liam found it very difficult. It was only then that he realised that Rachel was not coming back and he found it very hard to understand. I tried my best to explain every detail to him, but he was so confused. He wanted to know why, if Heaven was such a fantastic place, we couldn't all go there to be with Rachel. He wanted to know why

Rachel couldn't come back, just for a little while and we could let
her go back again. He tried to figure out ways to get to Heaven –
he suggested a long ladder, an aeroplane – we were amazed at what
he thought of. Once, in the middle of the night, he came in to us
crying: 'I want Rachel, I want Rachel!' They had been so close and
he missed her so much.

Laura was very lonely too. After all, she was the only one who
had to face into an empty room every night. John and I had each
other, Bernard and Liam had each other, but Laura was on her own.
I spent as much time as I could with her and encouraged her friends
to call.

Bernard missed Rachel in his own way. He coped very well and
was very practical about everything, but I knew he was hurting and
I knew he was missing his sister. The following Sunday I organised
a small party for him to make up for the birthday he couldn't
celebrate.

For the first week or two we had some visitors. A lot of people
were afraid to come – they didn't know how to cope or what to say.
What people didn't realise was that I needed people to come and
talk to me about Rachel. I was bursting to talk about her. I spent all
my time sorting out the photos, getting negatives reprinted,
organising frames and reading the cards I had been receiving. I
couldn't concentrate on a single thing apart from Rachel. I went to
her grave every day, sometimes twice, organised her flowers and
made sure it was tidy. I felt that this was all I could do for Rachel
now, and it kept me going.

I found that some days were OK, especially if I was encouraged
by something special in the post, or a phone call or a visit from a
friend. But other days I would be so down and nothing would bring
me back up. These were what I called my 'bad days' and when I look
back on my little diary all I see is 'good day' or 'bad day'. I hadn't the
energy to write anything else. The two main changes I noticed
about myself during that time were firstly, the cold – I was
constantly shivering and always had this cold feeling, which is

associated with shock – and secondly, my lack of energy. I had no energy whatsoever and even if I did manage to start something, I usually had to abandon it halfway through as I wouldn't be able to concentrate. I lost all interest in work and wondered if I ever would get it back.

I can't stress enough how much the constant phone calls, letters, cards and prayers meant to me – they gave me great comfort and strength and I can never be thankful enough to those people who thought of me and took the time to contact me. I have a couple of close friends who were very good to me and one in particular who rang me every single day, sometimes twice, and called to see me three or four nights a week; she knew my bad days without me telling her, she took me out to lunch when I needed cheering; she bought me a thermal vest when I couldn't get warm; she sat with me even when I wouldn't talk and she was the best kind of friend anyone could ever wish for. I don't know how I would have got through that difficult time without her and she is still there for me and hopefully always will be. It's at times like these that you realise who your real friends are!

Of course, without John I wouldn't have come as far as I have. John had lost his mother and his daughter within eighteen months and he was hurting badly. Rachel's death hit him hard and as well as coping himself, he was very worried about me and so concerned about the effect Rachel's death would have on me. There were lots of times when we were a great help and comfort to each other, but also lots of times when we were both down and then we weren't any good to each other and these were the hardest times. We were both hurting so much and there were times when nothing could be said and we knew there was nothing we could do to make things right again. There are statistics to prove that parents who have lost a child have more chance of splitting up than parents who hadn't been through such a trauma. We can understand this! Thankfully, our marriage is strong and the deep-rooted love we have for each other gave us the strength we both needed to cope.

On the Friday, the week after Rachel died, I was so lonesome. We were back at her grave, and as we turned to come back a huge rainbow appeared in the sky. Now the rainbow really seemed to take on a special meaning to us and we all have seen so many rainbows since Rachel left us. Maybe we never noticed them before, but everyone associates a rainbow with Rachel now. I often get phone calls to look out the window and there would be a rainbow in the sky. Sometimes they were very faint, but sometimes they would be a semicircle across the whole sky. One particular Saturday I was driving to Kilrush to get flowers for the grave. I was on my own and shouldn't have been driving as I was crying and in a very bad way. Of course I should have rung someone, but at times like that I felt it was something I had to cope with and figured no-one could help me anyway. When I was halfway there, I looked in my mirror and there was this beautiful rainbow and it stayed with me all the way until I got to Kilrush. Afterwards I figured it was Rachel's way of minding me and not letting me crash. Several times, incidents like this happened and although I had doubts back then, I am convinced now that it definitely was Rachel's way of contacting me.

I put all my energy into Rachel by sorting out photos and frames and reading the cards. At first I couldn't pray, but later on I did. I had received several special little books and leaflets and prayers and I would read through them at night. I felt that it brought me a little closer to Rachel. I figured if there was really a Heaven then Rachel and God were there and if I gave up on prayer and God then I would be giving up on Rachel. I felt it was my only way of keeping in touch with her so I prayed as often as I could.

I started making enquiries about getting a little memoriam card done for Rachel. I had my mind made up that I wanted something special and different but didn't make much progress with my first enquiries. I couldn't imagine having the regular one done up for Rachel – it wouldn't have done her justice. Then I rang up a company in Cork who said they did bookmarks. First I said no, but then they said I would have to see them so I agreed to look at some samples. The following morning a package arrived with about five or six samples of bookmarks for children – they were so beautiful and sad and I cried and cried reading them and looking at the photos. The first one was of a little girl aged ten named Rachel. I knew straight away that this is what I would do for our Rachel and rang them up immediately and found them so nice and helpful. I had to choose five or six of my favourite photographs, a verse and whatever else I wanted on the card, and they said they would do me up a draft within a couple of weeks. I set to work on this and everything was ready the following day. The verse I choose was the 'Rainbow' verse – the one that was given to us at the hospital, and I had no problem picking the photos.

It was very difficult without Rachel. Everything reminded us of her. We missed her in the mornings, when the others came in from school, in the evenings, at night-time, just all the time. Her stuff was all over the place, her school bag, her runners, her jacket in the hallway, her toys and books, and of course her room was still her room. Laura and I went through all her clothes one night. Rachel used to have a few favourite things to wear and everything else was just left in the wardrobe. I often used to give out to her for wearing the same stuff over and over again when she had new clothes just hanging there. So it was hardest seeing the tracksuit bottoms and the tops that she had worn so recently. There were lots of little belly tops that she was just starting to like and there were a lot of Laura's clothes that she had been looking forward to wearing. We sorted it all out and made up different piles. I held on to a few special things and the following evening we called Niamh over and we gave her a lot of clothes. She was delighted to get them. We also gave some to her cousins. The hardest thing of all was finding the little notes all over the place. She was forever writing letters and even now I sometimes find one and they are so special.

When the month was up we had to organise a Mass, as is traditional. There were times when I was coping OK, but most of the time I was in very bad form and found this was putting me under pressure. There was no way I wanted a house full of people again and to have to go through all the fuss of the previous month. I just couldn't cope with it. I told my family at home my views, that I didn't want them coming down. At first they were surprised, but afterwards they understood it from my point of view and had their own Mass especially for Rachel in their local church, and there was a great turnout for it. I felt I made the right decision and we had our own Mass and we got through it OK.

By then it was 12 December, and Christmas was the next event we had to get through. I dreaded it so much. I knew I wouldn't be sending any cards, my first time ever. I knew I would have to get presents for the kids, but that would be my limit. The first time I went to Ennis to do some shopping I nearly cracked up. I went into Penney's and there was Christmas music playing and all the mothers were going around full of excitement and enthusiasm and I just couldn't take it. I left crying and had to come home without anything. We decided to make a bit of an effort by putting up some decorations for Liam and Bernard and Laura, but I'm afraid it wasn't too successful. Normally when John picks the Christmas tree, he does so very carefully and it takes him ages to choose one that is just right. That year, he picked the first one that was shown to him and he brought it home and no matter what we put up on it, it still looked so bare and lonely.

I must say that everyone was very good and made a huge effort to make it special for the kids, especially the boys. They got loads of extra presents. My cards were still coming in – not one day passed without one or more and then the Christmas cards came – most of them really beautiful and so special. People went to so much trouble picking these thoughtful cards and I appreciated them so much.

That year was also special on account of the millennium. There were so many things organised to make it a special night. The end of one century and the beginning of another! The previous year we had stayed in on New Year's Eve and had a lovely night. Up to that myself and John had usually gone out and left the kids with a babysitter. However as the girls were getting bigger we decided not to leave them and we opened a bottle of champagne and had a little party for the kids and we all had a great night. The millennium was discussed and the kids were asking us what we would be doing the following year. We told them that no matter what we were doing, we would all be together on that special night – I made that promise to them. Unfortunately, it was a promise I couldn't keep.

So we got through Christmas. It was very sad and lonely especially at Mass on Christmas Eve and, of course, at home on Sunday morning. Rachel was missed more than ever but we got on with things. We saw in the New Year together and the next thing we had to cope with was Rachel's birthday, which was on 10 January. She would have been eleven. On that morning I lit a candle for her in the kitchen and kept it burning all day. I went over to the grave after dropping the boys to school and cried and cried. I didn't think I would be as bad but found it so hard. I met Niamh there, who was also heartbroken. As the day went on, things improved. I got so many special cards and even a bunch of flowers. Everyone remembered what day it was and it actually turned out to be celebration for Rachel's birthday instead of a sad day. I am sure she helped me and I felt she was happy. Since Rachel died, I have noticed that the special and important days can actually be happy days, but I have also realised that the following day is always bad – sort of an anti-climax. It is like as if I am on a high, acknowledging Rachel for a while, but that can't last and I go down so bad afterwards. However back to those first days of 2000 when, a week after Rachel's birthday, John's birthday and my own followed. It was the first time ever that I didn't want to acknowledge my birthday, but once again, family and friends made an effort and I had a nice day.

Another difficult day to get through was our visit back to the hospital to speak to the doctor and get the results of the post-mortem. Nuala had kept in touch with us on a regular basis and had organised this appointment for us. She had been absolutely fantastic, ringing us several times before, during, and after Christmas and on Rachel's birthday. We were both very nervous heading back to the hospital. I was hoping we wouldn't be brought to the parents' room where we had so many sad memories and was thankful when Nuala met us and took us upstairs, where we hadn't been before, to meet the doctor. He seemed totally different – much more relaxed. We realised afterwards that it had been very difficult for him when Rachel was so sick – it was hard for him to be relaxed when he knew there was nothing he could do to save our daughter.

He had Rachel's file with him and went through everything that had happened since Rachel was taken to Dublin. He told us that the post-mortem didn't really show up that much, but did confirm that Rachel died from encephalitis, which is a virus in the brain and that the exact virus is not know. He showed us a model of a brain and pointed out the part that was damaged by the virus. He assured us that nothing could possibly have been done that would have made any difference to Rachel. He explained to us that she had got a very common virus in her system. With the majority of people, the virus leaves with or without antibiotics; however with Rachel, the virus travelled to her brain and was destined to kill her brain from the very start. It attacked very fast. Some patients have encephalitis for long periods of time, but with Rachel it was unusually fast – she had no chance at all. We asked him loads of questions and he was very patient with us. He assured us that there was no possibility of the other children picking up the same virus, which was something I had been worried about. He said that what happened to Rachel was like a bolt of lightening – the chances of something like that happening again would be one in a million. Rachel was very unlucky.

He also told us that they would be keeping Rachel's file open and that I could ring him any time if I wanted any more information or had any queries. Apparently they are constantly doing research on the various viruses so it is possible that at some stage they might be able to put a name on Rachel's actual virus.

We came away feeling almost relieved. There was no-one to blame. Everything had been done. Rachel didn't suffer. She was so sedated that she wouldn't have felt anything. We are not sure whether or not she could hear us, but we like to think she could.

So, in the space of three months we had Rachel's sickness, her death and funeral, her month's mind, Christmas, New Year, her birthday, our birthdays and the visit back to the hospital. It was like being on a roller-coaster without the fun! If one was to ask me how I coped during those first few months, it would be hard to answer as it was all so different, some good days, but so many bad days. I used to worry an awful lot about the others and panicked if one of them was back late. I overreacted to every situation and poor Laura had to put up with a lot. I was constantly worried about them and it caused an awful lot of arguments between us. Probably my very worst time was about three weeks after Rachel died. About six months previous to that we had organised tickets to see Cher in concert in Dublin. We had also booked into a hotel and had a nice weekend planned. Of course, we had no idea back then what was ahead of us. Anyway, when the time came, we had no more interest in going, but my friends knew about it and encouraged us to go and said it would do us good to get away. They organised the kids for us so there was nothing stopping us. But when the time came, I just couldn't make the decision to go – I felt so low and rotten and at long last instead of heading off to Dublin, I got into bed and stayed there for a full day. This was something I had been threatening to do for a long time, but really, it didn't do any good and I felt more rotten afterwards. I know now I should have gone, but that was one of the times I hit rock-bottom and at least I realised that hiding under the quilt isn't the answer!

Shortly after Rachel died John and I had many conversations about the different places we had been to when Rachel was alive and we both knew we were lucky to have had so many special memories. Anywhere the children had wanted to go, or anything they wanted to get, we did our very best – within reason, of course – to facilitate. We knew we couldn't have done more for them. However, there was one regret that bothered us. When the girls were small, Disneyland opened in Paris and we decided that we would bring them there at some stage. We made a plan that when Laura would be ten, Rachel eight, and Bernard six, that would be the right time to go. However in the meantime, I got pregnant with Liam so that plan had to be postponed. They used to joke with me and warn me not to get pregnant again or else we would never get to go to Disneyland. I told them that as soon as Liam was out of nappies we would definitely go and it was something that was constantly discussed and looked forward to. In fact the summer before Rachel died, Liam was fully toilet-trained and that August I did call to the travel agents for brochures for February, but they told me to call back in a couple of weeks as they didn't have them there at that time. So the plan would have gone ahead, but obviously it wasn't meant to happen for Rachel.

So, after she died we made a decision that the five of us would go to Paris. I'm not sure if this was the right decision or not, but at the time we felt it would do us all good to get away. I rang the travel agents and of course one of the first questions the girl asked me was how many children I had, and I said four, but of course then I had to say three and I started crying and had to hang up. So that wasn't a great start, but eventually I got the holiday booked. We decided on a week altogether. The girl told me that a week would be too long in Disneyland itself so we decided to spend a few days in Paris city, something I had always dreamed of doing, although not under these circumstances. I left all the details to the travel agency and didn't dwell on it too much, but it cheered the kids up so much and we were happy to see smiles on their faces.

They had never been on a plane before and were so excited and it really did take their minds off things. The evening before we left, I went over to the grave and got so lonesome at the thought of 'leaving' her for a week, and the thoughts of actually going on holiday and Rachel not with us, put me into such a bad mood, I came back to the house, crying my eyes out. However within two minutes, two of my friends arrived to wish me luck – it was like Rachel had sent them to cheer me up and let me know it was OK to go – I felt much better.

The first part of the holiday in Disneyland was lovely – it is as magical as it appears on TV. We were all fascinated with everything and I will never forget the kids' faces when Mickey Mouse and the rest of them joined us for breakfast that first morning. Everything was so beautiful. We stayed in a lovely luxury hotel and I must say for a special treat it really is the place to go. The kids enjoyed every minute of it. Of course we missed Rachel and there were some tears shed and we knew she would have just loved it all.

We went on some spectacular tours, including the Louvre and the Eiffel Tower – right to the top – and we even went on a huge Ferris wheel. One day we were walking down the Champs Elysee – it was cold, but the sun was shining and I was feeling particularly lonesome. We stopped at three beautiful fountains and decided to take a couple of photos. All of sudden a fantastic rainbow appeared right in the centre fountain. We couldn't believe it – it is hard to describe it, but it was so beautiful and special – it was like Rachel's way of saying, 'Hi, I'm here too!' We took a photo of it and didn't know if it would come out or not, but it did and I have it framed upstairs in the hallway. Another day we had just left a restaurant and the kids had been given balloons. Liam let his go by accident and I thought there was going to be war as it disappeared up into the sky, but we told him that we were sending that one up to Rachel and to this day he remembers that and was glad to be able to 'give' her a present! So in general, it was a good holiday. Towards the end I was very anxious to get home, but I am glad we went and we have some good memories of our first holiday without Rachel.

That first year without Rachel was very difficult and probably the hardest year of my life. I can't say whether I dealt with it well or not as there is no 'proper' way to grieve. Every single person who is dealt a blow like this deals with it in their own way and it is such an individual thing, considering the various circumstances people find themselves in and their general attitude to life. There were some people that I could talk to, but with most people I believed that they couldn't understand and there was no point in trying to make them. At times, I preferred to be on my own, but then again, the more time I had to think and dwell on things, the more time I spent crying and in bad form. I found I had no patience with anyone, especially the kids. I found it very hard to be with happy, normal people and many times I had to get up and leave just because there was someone laughing or having a bit of fun. It took me a long time to learn to smile again and to feel happy.

There was a huge amount of pretending involved in my grief – putting on a face and saying everything was fine. This was easier than bursting out crying or moaning about my feelings. After a while, it actually got to a stage when I wasn't sure myself whether I was still pretending or if I was showing my true feelings. I was so mixed up and there are parts of that first year that I can't remember clearly, as I was so frustrated with myself. I used to feel like my head was going to explode and my heart was slowly breaking. I used to wonder if I would ever return to some kind of normal life.

We all missed Rachel so much. I missed her at the school in the mornings and at 3 o'clock when I would sit in the car to wait for Bernard and I would imagine what it would be like to see her running out to me. I was constantly wondering what it would be like if she was still alive and how she would react to different situations. I used to get angry sometimes when I reckoned that she was missing out on all the family occasions; particularly for Laura's birthday in June, Liam's in August and Bernard's in November. During that first summer without her I was so lonesome when I saw her friends heading over to the beach in their shorts and tee-shirts as I knew she would have been off on her bike and making the most of the holidays. That September was very difficult as she would have been heading off to national school for her last year and she wasn't there for the routine photographs.

At the beginning of October, John, Laura, Bernard and Liam and I headed up to Dublin one Sunday to Temple Street Hospital to join Nuala, the staff, and the parents of other children who had died during the previous year for a special service in memory of them all. Fifty-three children had gone to Heaven from June 1999 to June 2000. They ranged from newborn babies to teenagers. It was the most beautiful service with special prayers, songs, readings and hymns. They had a room done up with loads of candles, and flowers and soft toys. It was so beautiful and so sad. We all cried for our own children. It was so special and it meant an awful lot to us that Rachel and the others were being acknowledged in such a special way. They had done up a beautiful booklet with all the children's names and I will treasure that always. Each child's name was read out and a little night-light was lit. We were able to take this night-light with us when we went home. Also there was a little tree with a small hand painted rocking horse with each child's name on it, hanging off the branches – we were able to bring home Rachel's one and we decided that we would hang this on our Christmas tree each year. Afterwards we could have gone to the canteen for tea and met up with some of the other parents, but we were emotionally drained and I couldn't face that canteen – it had too many bad memories. However we were really glad we went and it was great for Laura and the boys to realise that they weren't the only ones to lose a brother or sister.

Keeping Rachel's Memory Alive

It was on my mind that Rachel's class had only one year left in national school before they split up and headed to secondary school. I wanted to do something special in the school before they left. I had heard about parents planting trees or a rose bush, but I knew this wouldn't work in our case. I thought about this for a long time and eventually came up with an idea that would keep me going for the rest of the year.

I planned to have a 'Day for Rachel' in the school before her first Anniversary and before her class left the school so I spoke with the teachers and the priest and we organised it for 27 October which would be a year after Rachel went into hospital. We decided that we would have a special Mass with all the kids taking part, and I had a few different ideas about how we would celebrate Rachel's life. Once I started thinking about it, I became almost excited and put great detail into the planning of it. I just knew it would be a very special day and it gave me something to dwell on and concentrate on and it made me feel close to Rachel while I was doing this.

Regarding the special bookmarks we had done for Rachel, I had started sorting these as soon as they came, which was some time in January. I wrote a little note on each one and used the many Mass cards and letters to help me. I used to write a few every night. I know that I should have done them with someone. There was no shortage of offers of help from my friends, but it was something I wanted to do myself. It was a difficult task and I spent many nights crying over them and trying to choose the right words for the special people in my life, like my family, my close friends, but most of all Rachel's friends and class mates. Eventually I got them all done – I never actually counted them but there were several hundred altogether. The bulk of them went in the post, but I decided to hand deliver a lot of them and I set aside a particular Monday to do this.

I started off with the school. I had done out a little card for each of the children in fifth and sixth class and one each for the teachers. I asked permission to speak to the kids for a few minutes and I will never forget how nervous I felt and how my heart was thumping when I walked into that room and saw all of Rachel's friends looking up at me. I gave them each their envelope and then tried to sound strong and told them all what happened to Rachel. My strength didn't last too long and before I knew it there was a lump in my throat and a shake in my voice. I had to give up. Of course all the children had started to cry as well and I felt so stupid. I told them that they could come to me at any time to ask me questions or talk to me about Rachel and then I left. I felt so bad for having upset them. However, later on I was so glad that I did. I found out that it meant an awful lot to each of the children, and they were thrilled to be given a card of their own, which I think they will treasure forever. Their teacher told me later that they cried for a while, but that this was good for them to show their emotions and at break-time each of them opened their envelopes and felt important to have one for themselves.

After the school, I visited each of my friends and gave them their cards. I cried with everyone and found it to be a very emotional day. The response was overwhelming. Everyone thought that the cards were so beautiful and were a fantastic tribute to Rachel. To this day, most houses I go into, I see Rachel's card up somewhere, on a mantlepiece, in a frame, or stuck on a fridge, and this means so much to me and I am so glad I chose those particular people to help me.

Around this time, John and I had another idea that we made enquiries about. We thought about getting a portrait of Rachel done.

We knew nothing about portraits, but through a mutual friend we got in touch with an artist and when we told him our story he put us in touch with his wife. After meeting her, we knew straight away that she was the person who would take on this special project for us. She came to visit us one Sunday afternoon and spent a couple of hours hearing all about Rachel's life and looking at her photos. It was as if she was trying to get to know Rachel. Catherine was her name and we all got on so well, she was so special and I am glad to have had the privilege of working with her. She picked out two photos that she thought suitable and asked me would I be able to get my hands on the negatives. One of these photographs was taken by a professional a couple of years previously and the other was taken by friends of ours from America who were home on holidays the year before. I told Catherine I would do my best and set about immediately trying to locate the negatives.

After a couple of weeks, my friends from America contacted me to tell me they had found the negative. I couldn't believe it. They told me that they had a big bag of old negatives and they went through every single one of them and found the important one down at the bottom. They came home in June and not only did they bring the negative, but also the most beautiful picture which they had done for me from the negative and they had it framed – it was a close-up of Rachel with a background of leaves and it really is beautiful. I have it in the kitchen and I was so touched that they had gone to this trouble for me. Once again I am lucky to have so many special friends.

Catherine said she would be ready to start on the portrait in September and hopefully have it ready for Rachel's first anniversary. She called a couple of times during the summer and took some pictures of Laura, Bernard, Liam and Malty and spoke to us about what we would like as a background. We told her we would like the rainbow in the portrait and left the rest up to her. We respected her judgement and were fairly confident that she would do a good job and do justice to Rachel.

Another picture formed part of 'A Day for Rachel'. We had arranged for a special picture of Rachel, which we were going to put in the hallway in the school. It was the same photograph that we used for the portrait, but this time it was transferred by computer on to a metal background, on a timber plaque. We had her name printed on it with her date of birth and the length of time she spent in the school and an appropriate verse. It turned out just beautiful and we arranged to have it ready for 27 October.

I planned to have the Mass with Fr Larkin at 10 o'clock and the teachers went to great effort with the children and all of them would participate. They chose some beautiful hymns, including 'Seasons in the Sun', 'Circle of Friends' and many more. They did up a little booklet and we chose some of Rachel's special things for the offertory procession. After the Mass I intended showing the kids some videos I had of Rachel, including the one of her First Holy Communion. Then we were going to give out some sweets and drinks so they could have their 'party' and following that, Fr Larkin was going to take the older classes aside and talk to them regarding Rachel and answer any questions that they might have. The final part of the day would be releasing helium balloons up in to the sky to Rachel. I was very nervous coming nearer to this special day, but felt confident that it would go well and felt I owed it to Rachel to do this for her. I was constantly afraid that Rachel would be forgotten and I just had to do everything in my power to keep her memory alive after her death.

Somehow, we got through the difficult times, and before we knew it the year was almost up. The special day for Rachel on 27 October was just beautiful and special. I was so nervous as I didn't know what to expect or how the kids would react but, as it turned out, there were far more tears of laughter than tears of sorrow. Fr Larkin said the Mass at 10 o'clock. We had the room done up beautifully with a little table full of special pictures of Rachel and other little mementoes. We had the helium balloons all around and the sun was beaming in the windows. The children sang lovely hymns and songs and they all did their little readings and prayers so well. Fr Larkin gave a lovely sermon and spoke about Rachel and it was almost impossible to be sad – it is hard to describe the feeling that was in the room that morning, but it was definitely filled with an air of joy and happiness and sunshine. After the Mass I put on some home videos of Rachel – the first one was of her First Holy Communion, which would have been about two and half years previous to this. Well, they all laughed so much to see themselves and to hear themselves. They thought it was hilarious and they got such a kick out of it. Then I showed one with Rachel and Niamh at home, dancing and singing and they were off in fits of laughter again. I was delighted to see this response. The next stage was the party and we gave out crisps and sweets and drinks and then we left the smaller kids to watch cartoons and Fr Larkin took the bigger classes aside to have a talk with them regarding Rachel. John and I sat in on this and hadn't a clue what their reaction would be. We needn't have worried, as once again, Fr Larkin handled it so well and encouraged them so much that there wasn't enough time for them all to say what they wanted to say. It was a great chance for them to express themselves and once again, there was lots of laughter and many funny memories from some of them.

The time went by so quickly, and when 12 o'clock came we cut the strings on the balloons and gave one to each child. We all ran outside and counted down from ten to one and they let go of the balloons. They went up and up and up into the clouds and we watched them until they disappeared. It was the most beautiful sight and even though there were tears in most of our eyes, we were filled with such happiness and joy, especially myself, and looking back I know there was only one person responsible for everything going so well and that was Rachel herself. She was with us and I felt so close to her and I felt she was proud of us for going to so much trouble.

I was on a high for a few days after that and lots of parents told me afterwards that their kids found the day to be so special and I knew I had done the right thing. It was another way of acknowledging Rachel and keeping her memory alive. Her special picture was also put up in the hallway of the school that day and it is still there and hopefully will be for a long time. We took a video of the Mass and took some nice pictures of Rachel's classmates around her table and those are very special to me now. After the Mass the children presented myself and John with two special gifts. The first one was a page written by each of Rachel's classmates and put together by their teacher. Each child wrote down whatever they felt about Rachel, their own special memories, a poem, a prayer, a picture or whatever they felt like. The second one was a large scrap book, again, a page each for all the other children in the school. Each of them paid their own individual tribute to Rachel, even the very young ones. Now these two 'books' are so very precious to us. Of course, I cried loads the first time I read them and also laughed as some of them are so funny and there are even little stories about things that happened at school that I didn't know about, and never would have known if the children hadn't been given a chance to put their thoughts and memories on paper. I will be forever grateful to the teachers who organised this and I will treasure those pages always. I often take them out and read them over and over again and I find it another way to feel close to Rachel.

For her actual anniversary I also planned a very special Mass. I reckoned whatever I did had to be done within the first year as I thought once that was over, I wouldn't be able to continue to go on doing these special things. I had asked my cousin Fr Aquinas to come down and say the Mass and despite being very busy in his parish in Dublin he did come down, which meant a lot to me. Most of my own family came too and the church was packed on that Sunday morning at 9 o'clock. All her friends from school and Lahinch were there and the teachers had organised a lovely choir. All my family participated and it was so special. At the end, I read out something that Aquinas had given me shortly after Rachel died and which gave me great comfort*. I had read it myself about a

*'A Comforting Prayer'. Printed on p103.

hundred times, but to a lot of people in the church it was their first time hearing it and it created a lot of tears.

Once again, I had organised the helium balloons and we took them to the grave and after some prayers we let them off and it was just fantastic. It meant so much to Liam and all the younger ones. We had a nice day after that – a lovely get-together for our two families. Rachel's celebration of her first birthday in Heaven went really well with so many prayers and good wishes from so many people in the form of cards, letters, phone calls, and visitors.

Of course, a couple of days later the usual anti-climax hit me with full force and I went down very badly – this always happens to me and I think it always will. A bad period after a special day. However I had organised a party for Bernard's birthday as he had missed out the previous year and that took my mind off things although I always miss Rachel really badly on the birthdays.

Shortly after this Catherine, the artist, rang us to tell us the portrait was ready. It had taken her a little longer than planned, but we didn't mind, as we didn't wish to put her under pressure. We went straight to her house to pick it up and were so delighted with it. It was perfect. The likeness was unbelievable in relation to Rachel and also to the other three and even Malty. The rainbow was there of course and Rachel herself looked so life-like, we couldn't stop staring at it. We took it home and hung it that night. Some of our friends came to see it and everyone thought it was just beautiful and so special. It's as if part of Rachel is here with us in the room and I will forever be grateful to Catherine for putting so much effort into it and for doing such a fantastic job.

Time Moves On

Then it was time for Christmas again. I couldn't believe we were facing a second Christmas without Rachel. This time I knew we had to make more of an effort than the previous year so we put up a proper tree and decorations and even though Mass on Christmas Eve was very lonely and Christmas morning was sad without Rachel, we did manage to get through it and the kids did enjoy themselves. I cried lots of times, but mostly when I was on my own. Sometimes I would look back over the photo albums knowing well that I would cry, but when I cried I felt closer to Rachel. This probably sounds so silly but that is the way I felt for a long time. I used to look at the videos also. There was one particular one that we took a year before Rachel died when we rented out a boat and went up the Shannon. Liam just loved watching this one and the two of us would watch it over and over again.

During this time I became very anxious about Laura, Bernard and Liam whenever they were out. I worried all the time, especially if they weren't back at the organised time, even if I knew where they were and who they were with. I had these panic attacks and used to freak out so many times. I used to imagine all sorts of things and sometimes could only relax when I had the three of them safely at home with me. This caused all sorts of problems and I know now that I totally over reacted to these situations. The same thing happened if one of them got sick, even a regular cold or a bug, or if one of them got hurt. I suppose at the back of my mind I thought more bad things were going to happen and I used to get so stressed about it.

Speaking of stress, I went through a very bad period when I was completely stressed out, very tired all the time and clinically depressed. I will never forget the tiredness that I experienced. I thought that there must be something seriously wrong with me and I went to the doctor and had every type of blood test done, but thankfully I got a clear bill of health apart from my depression, which was partly due to my bereavement. I tried anti-depressants, I tried counselling, but neither really worked for me. Eventually I got things sorted out in my head and very slowly, the tiredness started to go away.

I think that I never will be the same person I was before Rachel died. Everything has changed so much. I have gone through a lot of different stages of grief over the past two years and I know that I couldn't have avoided any one of them. I probably still have more to go through, as I think when you lose someone close to you, you spend the rest of your life learning to cope with that loss. However, I do believe that I have come a long way and even though I am not fully at peace with myself, I think I will get there some day.

In the beginning, I hadn't a clue where Rachel was. I kept asking her over and over again and of course got no answer. I wondered if she was just over in the graveyard, her body just bones, and that was the end of that. I wondered if she was in this famous place called Heaven and imagined what it was like. I begged her and begged her to give me a sign and I'm sure there were plenty at the time, but I was blind to them all. I made myself a little prayer book, made up of all the little prayers I had collected over the years and I put all the special notes that people had given to me and I cut out little photos of Rachel and stuck them on the cover. I also kept memoriam cards of people I knew so I had a bundle of stuff and used to take them all out every night and read through them. I reckoned that if there really was a God, then Rachel must be with him so I knew that if I said my prayers this was like keeping in with God and therefore my only way of keeping in touch with Rachel. I wasn't sure if I was doing the right thing or not, but I kept it up.

I also had two special boxes. In one, I kept all the beautiful cards and letters that I received after Rachel died. I still look back on them sometimes. In the other one I keep some of Rachel's own special things, like the book the hospital gave me, her First Holy Communion book, some of her school copies, a little diary she kept (that is so funny!), several of her little letters to me that I have found since, and many more little things that mean so much to me. Again, I often open this box and go through everything and have a little cry to myself.

There have been so many moments of grief that we shared as a family, but as well as those there also have been many moments that were my own personal feelings and these were very difficult to cope with. Before Rachel left us she was really into the set dancing and had just mastered the 'batter', and I know for certain she would have gone on to make an excellent dancer. After she died I found it impossible to watch any one set dance, in particular the children. If I found myself in a room where there was dancing I would have to leave and would always have a cry for myself. Some of the local little kids who were learning used to often call me to show me their steps and I just couldn't watch them. This was so hard for other people to understand, but for me it was very painful. I knew that I would have to overcome this somehow, so I made a decision after the first anniversary to start Liam off at the set dancing classes as soon as he was old enough. Everyone always said that he took after Rachel, so maybe he would be a good dancer too and I felt that Rachel would like the idea of Liam taking over where she left off. So in September 2001, I took Liam down to the classes. My heart was pounding and I felt scared, but we got through it and Liam loved it. Not only that, but the following week when it was time to go, Bernard decided that he wanted to go too. I was so surprised as Bernard never expressed an interest in dancing and I didn't think he would like the idea of being in a class with kids three and four years younger than him. However, he loved it and now the two of them head off every week and I am so proud of them. I often get a lump in my throat when I see the children dancing, particularly the little girls and I will never forget the evening they were learning to batter, I completely broke down and had to leave. I am sure there will always be reminders to make me feel lonesome and sad, but I don't mind too much. Sometimes crying helps me feel close to Rachel.

Another time during that first year I called to see a little girl I know who was sick in bed. A normal little girl with a normal sickness. Just like Rachel in the early stages of her sickness. The only difference, of course, being that this little girl, like most kids, got better and Rachel didn't. I left that bedroom and went home and cried and cried and cried at the unfairness of it all. Of course the guilt and remorse followed, but it is only natural to be envious of other situations.

Since Rachel's death, I have met and become friendly with a lot of special people. I have also read up on various subjects relating to life after death, spiritualism and related topics. I would never have read books like that before, but because of Rachel, I get huge comfort from these books and even though I have a lot of unanswered questions, I do seem to have a better understanding of things. I do believe that Rachel is out there somewhere and she knows what we are doing and what will happen in our lives. In the beginning, I think I expected too much from her and expected her to solve all my problems. I was constantly looking for proof that she could hear me and used to get so angry when I got no response or no sign. Now I realise that I was looking too hard and, really, the signs were there, but I was blind to them. I know that each of us come into this world, born with a free will. God, or Rachel, or whoever else is up there can't make this a perfect world for us – they have to let us make our own choices. Circumstances and events affect our lives and if they were to 'fix' all our problems with their 'magic wand', then we wouldn't learn from our mistakes. We have to make the most of our lives here and try and sort things out as best we can.

However, I still know and believe that Rachel is out there somewhere and maybe she will do something someday to prove that one hundred per cent, and maybe she won't – I don't mind now. I can't spend the rest of my life waiting and wondering – that wouldn't do my family or me any good at all! I think I am getting a clearer picture of the way things are. Of course I miss Rachel and constantly wonder what would she be doing now if she were alive. I get upset for Laura and the boys and John who miss her desperately and I wish to God that poor Rachel was not the unlucky one-in-a-million to get this virus in the first place, but things happen, good and bad and we have to accept them. After all, when something brilliant happens like a healthy little baby is born, we don't question it, we accept it and that is what we have to do when the bad things happen too. It is a bit like a test for us – how do we react and cope when tragedy strikes?

Most people say that time heals. Time does not heal, but it does make a difference. For the first year after Rachel died I think I was on a bit of high and I was allowed to grieve. By this I mean that I had so much going on in my head – planning various things to help keep Rachel's memory alive and this helped me get thought those awful months. When I say I was allowed to grieve, I mean people didn't mind me being in bad form and had such patience with me. I found all this changed once the first anniversary was over. I couldn't keep on organising things – I had it all done. And I found that I was expected to get on with my life and I couldn't share my feelings as I had done before. So I found myself in situations where my tears were my own and did most of my crying alone. I would be driving along sometimes and the memories would come to me and I would cry so much. This still often happens.

It is now just after Rachel's second anniversary. I can't believe that I have survived two years without her – it has gone by so quickly and yet it seems like ninety-two years since I last saw Rachel running in the door or heard her voice, so time is a funny thing. People often ask me how I am – it is hard to answer that truthfully, as I know I have come a long way in the last two years and yet it still feels as if there is part of me missing. I think I will just have to get used to that.

I know that Rachel will always be part of our lives, just not in the same way as Laura, Bernard and Liam. I will continue my efforts to keep her memory alive and I hope that whoever reads this will get some idea of what Rachel was like during her short life. I think it must be the worst possible thing to happen to any parent and I hope and pray that I won't have to experience it for a second time. However, there are times when I feel so close to Rachel and I feel she really is my angel watching over me and I am thankful for this special relationship.

Prayers and Poems

A COMFORTING PRAYER

To my dearest family,
Some things I'd like to say,
But first of all to let you know
That I arrived OK.

I'm writing this from Heaven,
Where I dwell with God above
Where there's no more tears or sadness,
There is just eternal love.

Please do not be unhappy
Just because I'm out of sight;
Remember that I'm with you,
Every morning, noon and night.

That day I had to leave you
When my life on Earth was through
God picked me up and hugged me
And He said 'I welcome you.

'It's good to have you back again
You were missed while you were gone
As for your dearest family
They'll be here later on.

'I need you here so badly
As part of My big plan,
There's so much that we have to do
To help our mortal man.'

Then God gave me a list of things
He wished for me to do,
And foremost on that list of mine,
Is to watch and care for you.

And I will be beside you,
Every day, week and year,
And when you're sad I'm standing there
To wipe away the tear.

And when you lie in bed at night,
The day's chores put to flight,
God and I closer to you
In the middle of the night.

When you think of my life on Earth
And all those living years,
Because you're only human
They are bound to bring you tears.

But do not be afraid to cry,
It does relieve the pain;
Remember there would be no flowers
Unless there was some rain.

I wish that I could tell you
Of all that God has planned,
But if I were to tell you,
You wouldn't understand.

But one thing is for certain
Though my life on Earth is over,
I'm closer to you now
Than I ever was before.

And to my very many friends
Trust God knows what is best
I'm still not far away from you;
I'm just beyond the crest.

There are rocky roads ahead of you
And many hills to climb,
But together we can do it,
Taking one day at a time.

It was always my philosophy
And I'd like it for you too
That as you give unto the World
So the World will give to you.

If you can help somebody
Who's in sorrow or in pain,
Then you can say to God at night
My day was not in vain.

And now I am contented
That my life it was worthwhile
Knowing as I passed along the way
I made somebody smile.

So if you meet somebody
Who is down and feeling low
Just lend a hand to pick him up
As on your way you go.

When you are walking down the street
And you've got me on your mind
I'm walking in your footsteps
Only half a step behind.

And when you feel that gentle breeze
Or the wind upon your face
That's me giving you a great big hug
Or just a soft embrace.

And when it's time for you to go
From that body to be free
Remember you are not going
You are coming here to me.

And I will always love you
From that land way up above,
Will be in touch soon
P. S. God sends HIS LOVE.

🌿 🌿 🌿

RACHEL'S SONG

I'll be in the breeze
Which rustles in the trees,
When autumn days are here
The first winter snowflake
Which falls in this place
Will just be me kissing your face
When light gentle raindrops
Fall soft on your brow
I'll be whispering 'I'm with you now.'

The sunshine which bathes you
In its warm summer glow
Will be just me hugging you
And when spring comes around
I'll be easily found
In the flower you hold in hand.
So whatever the season
Please don't be too sad
And always remember
The seasons we had.

❀　❀　❀

OUR BRIEF RAINBOW

Rainbows appear only on dreary, rainy days.
They beautify the world for a few brief moments.
These moments, however, can be spectacular.
Rachel, you were our brief rainbow.

You entered our lives, Rachel, and stayed for
Just a short precious while.
Nonetheless, the memories of those moments when
You blessed us with delight and joy
Beauty and gentleness, happiness and sunlight
Are treasured memories for us.

Rachel, having had you with us,
You brought love into our lives,
And allowed us to share our love with you.
The gifts you shared with us,
Allowed joy and laughter to enter our lives.

Rainbows, however brief,
Make the world a brighter, lovelier place,
How grateful we are that we had you
Rachel, our brief rainbow.

❀ ❀ ❀